the Gospel for Today

R. A. TORREY

WHITAKER
HOUSE

Unless otherwise indicated, all Scripture quotations are taken from the King James Version of the Holy Bible. Scripture quotations marked (RV) are taken from the Revised Version of the Holy Bible. Scripture quotations marked (ASV) are taken from the American Standard Edition of the Revised Version of the Holy Bible

All bold type in Scripture is the emphasis of the author.

The Gospel for Today

ISBN: 978-1-60374-727-1
eBook ISBN: 978-1-60374-728-8
Printed in the United States of America

Whitaker House
1030 Hunt Valley Circle
New Kensington, PA 15068
www.whitakerhouse.com

Library of Congress Cataloging-in-Publication Data (Pending)

1 2 3 4 5 6 7 8 9 10 19 18 17 16 15 14 13

CONTENTS

PREFACE

Repeated and insistent demands for a new volume of evangelistic sermons have been coming to me from pastors, evangelists, and publishers. I have felt the force of these demands and at last am yielding to them in publishing this new volume of sermons.

These sermons were, for the most part, preached to my own congregation in Los Angeles in the past few months, and God, in His wondrous condescension, has seen fit to bless them with the conversion of a good many persons, the great majority of whom have been men from the ages of twenty-five to fifty; but there have been some men of riper years converted, even up to seventy or eighty years of age. There have also been some notable conversions among women. We have been greatly interested in the number of Jews and Roman Catholics who have recently made a public profession of accepting Christ in our after-meetings. Many of whom have afterwards united with our church, the Church of the Open Door. Not a few of those converted were formerly skeptics, agnostics, infidels, and atheists, and quite a number of "Christian Scientists."

The gospel presented in these sermons is the same gospel of a crucified Christ, a Savior from the guilt of sin, a risen Christ, and a Savior from the present power of sin, that we have been preaching throughout our entire ministry as pastor, and as evangelist in all parts of the world. We are certainly living in a New Day. The war[1] and its after-results have worked a radical transformation in the ethical and religious, as well as social and economic, outlook of the minds of the men and women of the present day; nevertheless, we find that the same gospel that was *"the power of God unto salvation"* before the War, and from the days of the apostle Paul (Romans 1:16), is the gospel that men will listen to and yield to today. All of these new gospels, the "social gospel" with the rest, are proving utterly ineffective in saving individual men or in lifting up communities. The *real* gospel, when preached in the power of the Holy Spirit, produces the same effects in individual lives today, and in the transformation of families and communities, that it has produced throughout all the centuries since our Lord Jesus Christ died on the cross of Calvary, rose again, and ascended to the right hand of the Father and poured out His Holy Spirit upon His people. Practical results prove that that gospel does not even need to be restated, though of course it is desirable to adapt the illustrations and method of argument to the thinking of our own day.

There seems to be a great religious awakening in Scotland and in some parts of Ireland and England, and there are indications here and there of an awakening in our own land. It cannot be denied that many pastors who are thoroughly evangelical and many of our most intelligent laymen are tired of some of the methods of evangelism that have been in vogue in our own country during the past few years, but this does not mean for one moment that they do not believe in evangelism or in true revivals. We seem to be ripe for a revival now, and it is hoped these sermons may prove helpful in promoting that greatly longed for and earnestly prayed for genuine revival. It is hoped that they may be helpful to pastors in their desire to become their own evangelists, that they may be

1. World War I.

helpful to those evangelists whom God has chosen, and that they may be directly used to the salvation of many souls, by being put in the hands of men, women, and children who are unsaved and need a Savior. It has been a great joy to the author of this book to receive letters from different parts of the world, from all classes of people, saying that they had been led to Christ through reading printed reports of his sermons.

In our own church, we have found that it has not been necessary to introduce movies, or other sensational features, to draw the crowds. We have never had a movie or anything of that kind in our church, and never expect to have; and yet our Sunday evening audiences at which these sermons were preached were probably larger than those of any other church in the community, even those resorting to the movies as a means of drawing a crowd; in fact, we think there is no other building used for religious services in the city that would hold the thousands of people who, Sunday night after Sunday night, have listened to these sermons. What the great attraction is to bring men and women to the house of God, as well as to bring them to a better life, is stated in the fifth sermon in this book.

—*R. A. Torrey*, Los Angeles, CA

1

A CONVERTED INFIDEL'S PREACHING

"And straightway he preached Christ in the synagogues, that he is the Son of God."
—Acts 9:20

You will find the text in Acts 9:20: *"And straightway he preached Christ in the synagogues, that he is the Son of God."* The Revised Version is even more suggestive, *"And straightway in the synagogues he proclaimed Jesus, that he is the Son of God."* There was perhaps never a more amazed audience than the one that heard Saul of Tarsus preach his first sermon in Damascus. Saul was known far and wide as a hater of Jesus Christ and as a persecutor of Christians. He had come to Damascus for the express purpose of laying waste to the church, arresting all believers in Jesus Christ, and dragging them to Jerusalem for punishment and death. On earth today, there is not and has not been for centuries, as bitter an infidel as Saul of Tarsus; and yet on his first public appearance in Damascus, this same Saul of Tarsus preached a sermon of tremendous power, declaring and proving that Jesus is the Son of God. Will you please look at two things tonight? If you will look at them earnestly and honestly, it will result in some of you being converted tonight. The first thing I wish you to look at is the preacher in the text. The second thing I wish you to look at is the preacher's message.

I. The Preacher

Look first at the preacher. The preacher was Saul of Tarsus. As you look at him, I wish to submit three good reasons why this particular preacher's message should command attention, and should be accepted. Taken together, these three reasons prove that the message is true beyond an honest question.

1. The first reason why this preacher's message should command attention and should be accepted is that *he had been a hater of the Jesus whom he now proclaimed.*

Saul had not been brought up to believe that Jesus was the Son of God, and therefore he did not keep on preaching it because it was what he had been taught to believe from childhood. There are many who say of our modern preachers, "Oh, he believes that and preaches that just because it is what his parents and early teachers taught him to believe." But no such charge can be brought against Saul of Tarsus. The doctrine that Jesus was the Son of God was not something Saul had taken up without any due thought, not something that he had inherited from his parents and early teachers.

Saul had opposed this doctrine with all the vigor of an intense soul; he had gone up and down the streets of the city of Jerusalem, in and out of the houses, arresting men, women, and children, for no other reason than that they believed that Jesus was the Son of God, and confessed their faith in Him as such. He had attended their trials and voted for their death. Nothing seemed to cause him greater joy than the violent death of a Christian. He had had a part in the murder of the first Christian martyr, Stephen. Not only so, but when he had exhausted all his opportunities of manifesting his hatred of Christians in Jerusalem in violent ways, his hatred of Christ and Christianity was not satisfied, and he had sought and obtained authority to go to Damascus to carry out a similar work of opposition and destruction there. Now when a man like that turns completely around and says, "I was wrong. I was utterly wrong. I was awfully wrong, in my denial that Jesus was the Son of God," then we ought to give his change of opinion careful attention; he must have had some good reason for it.

2. Saul's testimony ought to have great weight for another reason, and that is *because of what he sacrificed for his change of opinion.*

Saul's change of opinion cost him much. It cost him everything of a worldly character that he possessed. It cost him the loss of a position of great influence and promise. It cost him the loss of all his old friends. It cost him the severest persecution. It cost him arrest after arrest, imprisonment after imprisonment, scourging after scourging, stoning and insult, and attempted assassination. It cost him wandering, and hunger and nakedness. It cost him suffering of the most intense kind, and dangers of indescribable magnitude. When a man of standing and education like Saul of Tarsus makes sacrifices like that for a change of opinion, his new opinion must demand great consideration.

Of course, men are constantly changing their opinions because they are going to gain something by the change. Many a Republican becomes a Democrat, and vice versa, many a Democrat becomes a Republican, because of some personal profit that is to come to them in one way or another from the change. Of course, a change of opinion in a case like that is not worthy of much consideration. There are professed Christians who have become infidels, outspoken infidels, because they could make money by the change, or because they had sinned, and the truth of Christianity was causing them pain of conscience, and they wished to save their consciences, or because of some other low end that was to be gained by the change of opinion.

When I was in Sydney, Australia, a man was urged to come and hear my address, but he replied that he took no stock in that sort of thing. He himself had been a preacher once, and a missionary, and had found that the whole thing was a humbug. I took occasion to look into the man's history, and I found that he had been a missionary, but that his change of opinion was not due to the fact that further information and study had shown him that Christianity was untrue, but because as a missionary he had gotten into trouble for his immorality. He was expelled from the mission, as he should have been, and in that way was led to change his opinion about Christianity and to accept infidelity. But when a man of great intelligence changes his opinion, and sacrifices everything that men hold clear, for that change, and is transformed in character by the change, and when the man who does thus change is a man like Saul of Tarsus, who became Paul the Apostle, any honest man will hesitate a long time before he says Saul was mistaken in the change.

3. But there is a third reason, and a better one yet, why Saul's opinion must have great weight. Indeed this reason is so absolutely conclusive, if we are thoroughly honest, we must say that Saul was certainly right in what he says, and that Jesus is as Saul said he was, *"the Son of God." That reason is found in the way in which Saul of Tarsus came to change his opinion.*

Why did Saul change from the opinion that Jesus was an impostor and blasphemer to the opinion that Jesus was the Son of God? Saul himself told us why he changed his opinion. He said it was because as he drew near to Damascus, where he was going to arrest the Christians and bring them to Jerusalem to be punished, at the noon hour, suddenly there shone around about him from heaven a great light, brighter than the light of the noontime sun. In that light, he saw the face and form of Jesus who was once crucified, now risen and glorified, and that he heard a voice saying unto him, "Saul, Saul, why persecutest thou me?" When he inquired who was speaking to him, the form there in the glory said, "I am Jesus of Nazareth, whom thou persecutes." (See Acts 22:6–8, 16–18; see also Acts 9:5–6.)

Now if Saul of Tarsus really saw Jesus there in the glory, and if Jesus said to Saul what Saul reports that He said, and if Saul was commissioned at that time, as he said he was, to be the authoritative representative of this same Jesus, then Jesus certainly is the Son of God. There remains no room for debate about that. But the question arises, Did Saul really see Jesus in this way and hear Him say the things he said He did? He either did, or else Saul was a liar and made the story up, or else he was mistaken and had sunstroke or something of that sort that he fancied was a reality.

Did he lie and make the story up? Such a supposition is incredible; there was no object for the lie. There was nothing to be gained by the lie, and there was everything to be lost by it. Men do not manufacture lies for the sake of sacrificing position, home, money, comfort, ease, reputation, love of friends, and everything dear to them in life. The supposition then, that Saul of Tarsus lied in this matter, is ruled out.

Was Paul the victim of delusion and fancy through sunstroke or a flash of lightning and peal of thunder (which he mistook for the voice of Jesus) or overwrought imagination, or something of that kind, so that he imagined that he saw something he did not see, and heard something he did not hear? To this we would say that the record and well-attested facts in the case make this explanation impossible. Not only did Saul see the light, but those who journeyed with him saw the light, so it could not have been Paul's imagination. And not only did those who journeyed with him see the light, but they also heard the voice, though they did not distinguish the message that was spoken. Furthermore, Paul was blind for three days, and that was no fancy.

Further, there was another man, Ananias, who saw Jesus in a vision, and this Jesus whom he saw in the vision said, *"Arise, and go into the street which is called Straight, and enquire in the house of Judas for one named Saul, of Tarsus: for, behold, he prayeth, and he hath seen a man named Ananias coming in, and putting his hands on him, that he might receive his sight"* (Acts 9:11–12). Ananias protested against going, saying, *"Lord, I have heard from many of this man, how much evil he hath done to thy saints at Jerusalem: and here he hath authority from the chief priests to bind all that call upon thy name"* (verses 13–14). But the Lord who appeared to him in the vision insisted upon his going and he obeyed. He found Saul where the Lord Jesus had told him in the vision he would find him, and he *"entered into the house; and putting his hands on him said, Brother Saul, the Lord,* ***even Jesus****, that appeared unto thee in the way as thou camest, hath sent me, that thou mayest receive thy sight, and be filled with the Holy Ghost"* (verse 17). And immediately scales fell from Saul's eyes, and he received his sight. There is absolutely no room for the theory of delusion and fancy on Paul's part here. Does someone say the whole story in Acts is a fiction? Let them study it. I challenge any honest lawyer or historical critic to study this story carefully and candidly, with the desire to find out whether it is truth or fiction, and see if this story does not bear the unmistakable marks of truth.

In the eighteenth century, rationalism had swept everything before it in England. There were very few, even among the clergy, who still believed in the supernatural, but there were some remains of faith in the miracles and in the historic accuracy of the Bible, so the rationalists of the day appointed two of their ablest reasoners to undertake a campaign for the destruction of what remained of faith in the supernatural—Lord Lyttleton, an able lawyer, and Sir Gilbert West, Clerk of the Privy Council. These two men planned a campaign for the destruction of belief in the supernatural. One of them said to the other, "If we are to destroy faith in the supernatural, there are two alleged incidents in the Bible that we must prove to be legend or myth. One is the alleged resurrection of Jesus Christ from the dead, and the other is the alleged conversion of Saul of Tarsus."

Lord Lyttleton said to Sir Gilbert West, "Well, I will take the story of the conversion of Saul of Tarsus as recorded in the Acts of the Apostles and show it is not historic fact but legend." And Sir Gilbert West replied that he would take the story of the alleged resurrection of Jesus Christ, and show that that was not historic fact but legend or myth. Then West turned to Lyttleton and said, "I will depend upon you for my Bible material, for I must confess that I am somewhat rusty in the Bible." Lyttleton replied, "I was intending to depend upon you for my biblical material, for I also am somewhat rusty in the Bible." Then one of them said, "Well, we must be candid, and therefore we must carefully study the records in the Bible." They met a number of times while they were preparing their books. On one of these occasions, Lyttleton said to West, "West, as I have been studying the record in the Bible, I have become somewhat shaken in my position." West replied, "Well, I am glad to hear you say it, for I confess that as I have been studying the records regarding the resurrection of Christ, I have become somewhat shaken in my position." But they went on and completed their books.

At a last conference, West said to Lyttleton, "Have you written your book?" He replied, "Yes, I have, but as I have studied the facts as presented in the Bible and applied to them the canons of evidence received in courts of law, I have become satisfied of the truth of the Bible record, and that Saul of Tarsus was converted just as it is recorded in the ninth chapter of the Acts of the Apostles." Then he added, "Have you written your book?"

"Yes," Sir Gilbert West replied. "I have written my book, but as I have sifted the evidence regarding the resurrection of Jesus Christ as found in the Bible, I have become satisfied that Jesus Christ *did* rise from the dead, just as recorded in the Gospels, and I have written my book on that side."

Anyone who will do what this gifted lawyer did, sit down to a careful study of the conversion of Saul of Tarsus, as related in three different places in the Acts of the Apostles and as referred to in the Epistles, with an honest desire to know whether it is truth or fiction, will be compelled to come to the same conclusion that Lord Lyttleton did.

We arrive, then, at this point—that Saul of Tarsus changed from a bitter infidel to a believer in Jesus Christ and preached that "Jesus is the Son of God," because Jesus Christ appeared to him in glory as the Son of God. Saul of Tarsus actually saw him, and Jesus Christ appointed Saul His authoritative representative. It has been absolutely settled, not as a theological speculation, but as an established historic fact, established by absolutely conclusive testimony and evidence, that Jesus is the Son of God.

II. The Converted Infidel's Message

We can now turn from a consideration of the preacher to a consideration of the preacher's message. What was the preacher's message? What was the message this converted infidel brought to the people of Damascus and brings to us today? His message can be summed up in one short sentence, "Jesus is the Son of God." Look at Saul as he stands there and proclaims it. There he stands, a man who a few days before had been a bitter hater of Jesus Christ and Christianity, a man who had stained his hands with Christian blood, a man who had come to Damascus for the express purpose of arresting men and women because they believed in Jesus of Nazareth as the Christ, the Son of God, and professed their faith in Him. Around him stood Jews and others who had heard of him as the bitterest enemy that the cause of Jesus Christ had, as a man who stopped at nothing in his efforts to stamp out Christianity, and to their amazement, he declared to them that this Jesus whom he had persecuted, he had found upon indisputable testimony to be the Son of God. But God Himself stands in this audience tonight proclaiming this same message. Let us look closely at this message.

1. Note first that *the message is not that Jesus is a good man, or even the best man that ever lived on this earth. No, the message is that* ***"Jesus is the Son of God."*** That is, that He is a man who stands absolutely apart from all other men, that while He is a man, He is more than a man. He is of divine origin, and partakes of all the attributes of Deity, and is to be honored and worshipped even as God the Father is honored and worshipped.

2. Note second, that *the message is not merely that Jesus is a great teacher, but that "Jesus is the Son of God."*

3. Note third, that *the message is not merely that Jesus is a perfect man, and our example, but that "Jesus is the Son of God."*

4. Jesus is the Son of God. What does that involve?

(A.) *It involves absolute and wholehearted trust in Him.* If Jesus is the Son of God, then I can trust Him absolutely and wholeheartedly. I cannot trust any man absolutely and wholeheartedly, no matter how good he may be. I could not absolutely and wholeheartedly trust any man. The Word of God is right when it says, *"Thus saith Jehovah; cursed is the man that trusteth in man"* (Jeremiah 17:5 RV). If Jesus is not merely man, if He is divine, if He is the Son of God, if

He is God manifest in human form, I can trust Him absolutely, and that is what He demands that I shall do. On the night before His crucifixion, He demanded of His disciples the same absolute trust in Himself that they put in God the Father. He said, *"Let not your heart be troubled, believe in God, believe also in me"* (John 14:1 ASV). As He is the Son of God, He had a right to make that demand, that men should put their absolute trust in Him. If He had been merely man, even the best of men, He would not have demanded that these men bring the curse of God upon their heads by putting their absolute trust in Him. But because He was the Son of God, and because He was God manifest in the flesh, He could say, *"Believe in God,* ***believe also in me.****"* And that is what He is saying to each of us tonight; that is what He is demanding of us tonight.

(B.) *Believing that Jesus is the Son of God involves that we not only trust Him absolutely and wholeheartedly in a general way, but that we trust Him specifically for salvation, for salvation from the guilt of sin, and salvation from the power of sin.* No matter how utterly lost we may be, no matter how many sins we may have committed, no matter how completely we may be in the power of sin tonight, as Jesus is the Son of God, and according to His own word died upon the cross of Calvary in our stead, He could, as the Son of God, make a perfect atonement for sin, and the moment we trust in Him our sins are all forgiven. Furthermore, as He is the Son of God, He has power to save us from the power of sin. Sin may be stronger than we are, and Satan may be stronger than we are, but they are not as strong as the Son of God, and this Son of God undertakes to save from the power of sin everyone who puts their trust in Him. He also said, *"If the Son therefore shall make you free, ye shall be free indeed"* (John 8:36). As the Son of God, He has power to set free from the power of sin anyone who puts their trust in Him.

(C.) *A real faith that Jesus is the Son of God involves the surrender of our life to Him.* If Jesus is divine, if He is the Son of God, if He is God made manifest in the flesh, we should surrender to Him all that we are and all that we have. That is what He demands of us and has a right to demand of us. Remember, Jesus is the Son of God! Have you made a surrender of your whole life to Him? If not, will you make that surrender tonight?

(D.) *Real belief that Jesus is the Son of God involves the surrender of our thoughts to Him.* If Jesus is the Son of God, He is infallible, and He can never be mistaken; therefore, if a person, no matter how learned he may be, no matter how high he may stand in circles of education and culture, says one thing, and Jesus, the Son of God, says another, no man who really believes that Jesus is the Son of God will hesitate one moment which to believe. I have surrendered my thoughts absolutely to the shaping and to the control of Jesus Christ. For I am convinced, I am absolutely sure, that He is the Son of God. I say to any man, "Do you dare to set up your poor miserable opinions against the plain declarations of the Son of God? If you do, you are a fool, and however much you may resent the statement, the day is coming when you will see that you are a fool. God grant that it may not come when it is too late to repent."

There is saving power in this doctrine that Jesus is the Son of God. It will save any man who believes it from the heart and acts upon it.

1. *This doctrine will bring eternal life to anyone who believes it, really believes it from the heart, and shows that he believes it by acting upon it.* The apostle John said in John 20:31, "*These are written* [that is, these things written in the gospel of John are written] ***that ye may believe that Jesus is the Christ, the Son of God; and that believing ye may have life through his name.***" We see here that through simply believing that Jesus is the Christ, the Son of God, believing it with the heart, believing it in such a way as leads us to take the steps involved in thus believing it, anyone who thus believes, obtains eternal life.

2. *Believing in this doctrine will also bring victory over the world.* John in his first epistle says, "*Who is he that overcometh the world but, he that believeth that Jesus is the Son of God?*" (1 John 5:5). The world has a mighty power, a power to blind our minds, a power to break our resolutions, a power to degrade our lives. The great mass of men and women are yielding to this power of the world. They are giving up their high ideals. They are compromising with things that their own consciences condemn, things that are low and debasing. The world, the spirit of the times, the ideas that rule in this world, which "lieth in the wicked one" (see verse 19), are making a mighty assault on the faith and moral principles and the conduct of us all. That assault is too strong for any of us to resist in our own strength, but there is a way of victory, by believing, really believing, that Jesus is the Son of God.

I believe that practically everyone in this audience tonight is convinced that Jesus is the Son of God; but being intellectually convinced of a thing is one thing, and really believing it from the heart, yielding our will to that which our mind accepts, is quite another thing. Will you tonight accept Jesus Christ as the Son of God? Will you take that attitude toward Him that you ought to take toward one that you know to be the Son of God? Will you from this time on trust Him absolutely? Will you trust Him through His atoning death for the pardon of all your sins? Will you trust Him daily for His divine power for deliverance from the power of sin? Will you surrender your life absolutely to Him? Will you surrender your thoughts to Him, for Him to be absolute ruler of your thoughts? It is up to each one of you to answer the question. You can say "yes" or "no," whichever you will. Which will you say?

2

A KEYNOTE OF THE BIBLE

"God is love."
—1 John 4:8

Our subject is, "The Keynote of the Bible." You will find the keynote of the Bible in my text. You will find the text in John 4:8, "*God is love.*" That is one of the shortest sentences ever written, and it is certainly one of the greatest and profoundest. It is inexhaustible in its meaning and in its scope. Men have been studying, scrutinizing, pondering, and digging into that sentence through the eighteen centuries that have passed since it was written, and they have not exhausted it yet. Thousands upon thousands of sermons have been preached upon that text, yet something new awaits every preacher who studies it and seeks to expound it. Thousands of volumes have been written by some of the world's greatest thinkers, devoted to the study, exposition, and application of that sentence, but it is as fresh and full as ever, and it is constantly yielding new treasures to each new century, and to each new explorer of its exhaustless wealth. Men and angels will ponder that sentence throughout the endless ages of eternity and not exhaust it.

The Book that contains that matchless sentence bears the unmistakable seal of having God for its Author. The golden truth of priceless worth contained in this sentence is singular to the Bible. All the philosophers in the world never discovered that stupendous truth until God revealed it and the Bible declared it. The world would never have known that *"God is love,"* had not God revealed the fact in His own Word. It is true that there are evidences of beneficent design in nature and in history, but nature and history have both been marred by Satan's work and by the entrance of sin into the world. Only the interpretation of history and that insight into the future of man and nature and Satan that the Bible gives enables us to see love reigning above all and through all. We hear much in these days of the profound truths contained in the teachings of the world's great philosophers of ancient and of modern times, in philosophers like Socrates, Plato, Aristotle, Seneca, Isocrates, Epictetus, Marcus Aurelius Antonius, and in the teachings of the great founders of religions like Buddha, Mohammed, Confucius, and Zoroaster; but in none of them do we find this great truth that *"God is love,"* nor anything akin to it, not until the Bible revealed it. We owe this truth wholly and solely to the Bible. We must go then to the Bible for the interpretation of this truth.

This sentence is the keynote of the entire Bible. It is the great fundamental thought of the Bible. If anyone were to ask me to put into one sentence what the Bible teaches, I could do it. And this would be the sentence, *"God is love."* From start to finish—from Genesis 1:1 to Revelation 22:21—the Bible is one great, ever-swelling anthem, and the theme of that anthem is, *"God is love."* God's love is the keynote of the whole Bible, of each one of the sixty-six books that make up the completed whole. It was the love of God that led to the Creation as described in the first chapter of Genesis. It was God's love that led to the banishment of Adam and Eve from the Garden of Eden when they fell, as recorded in the third chapter of Genesis. It was God's love that led to the promise of the Savior, the seed of the woman, immediately after Adam and Eve had fallen. It was God's love that led to the call of Abraham and Jacob to be a blessing first to their own descendants and ultimately to the whole human race. It was God's love that led to the bondage of Israel in Egypt and to their deliverance from that bondage when the time was ripe. It was God's love that led to the giving of the Law through Moses on Sinai, and it was God's love that led to the extermination of the Canaanites.

It was God's love that led to the planting of Israel in that land so wondrously adapted by its natural configuration and by its location in the then-inhabited world to be the training-place of the nation that would bring blessing to the whole earth, and from which the Savior would be born. It was God's love that shaped Israel's history through all their wanderings from Him. It was God's love that at last rooted Israel out of the land He had given them and scattered them through the earth. It will be God's love that restores them again to the land that belongs to them by eternal covenant, when the time is full. It was God's love that sent Jesus Christ to die for sinful men, to rise again from the dead, and to ascend to the right hand of the Father in the glory. And it will be God's love that will send Him back again to earth when the fullness of time for that greatest event in all this earth's history has come. Heaven and all its glories, hell and all its horrors, both have their origin in the love of God. Yes, "*God is love*" is the keynote of the Bible, the secret of history, the explanation of nature and the solution of eternity's mysteries.

I wish to call your attention to some of the ways in which the love of God is manifested. Of course, it would take many sermons to recount all the manifestations of the love of God, but we can look at some of them, though it would take all eternity to fully understand and appreciate even them.

I. God's Love Manifests Itself in His Ministering to Our Needs and Joy

This comes out again and again in the Bible. For example, our Lord Jesus, in expounding to His disciples their own duty, said in Matthew 5:44–45, "*Love your enemies,...and pray for them which...persecute you;* ***that ye may be the children of your Father which is in heaven:*** *for he maketh his sun to rise on the evil and on the good, and sendeth rain on the just and on the unjust.*" And in the Old Testament in Deuteronomy 32:9–12, we read, "*For the* Lord*'s portion is his people; Jacob is the lot of his inheritance. He found him in a desert land, and in the waste howling wilderness; he led him about, he instructed him, he kept him as the apple of his eye. As an eagle that stirreth up her nest, fluttereth over her young, spreadeth abroad her wings, taketh them, beareth them on her wings. So the* Lord *alone did lead him, and there was no strange* [foreign] *God with him.*"

This is a marvelous picture of the wondrous love of God that we cannot stop to go into in detail. Every blessing of life is a love token from God. As the Holy Spirit put it through the apostle James in James 1:17, "*Every good gift and every perfect gift is from above, and cometh down from the Father of lights, with whom is no variation, neither shadow of turning.*" When the sun shines with its warmth and light and gladness, lift up your head with joy and say, "This is a token of my Father's love." When you look upon the blossoming flowers, the growing grass, the budding trees in their spring beauty, say, "All this beauty with which God adorns the earth, this is another token of God's love to me." When you feel health and strength coursing through your veins, look up and thank God again for this another token of His love. The countless blessings that come to us all every day of our lives, most of them unnoticed in our blindness and ingratitude, are all tokens of His great and constant love.

II. God's Love Is Manifested in Chastening When We Forget Him, Wander Away, and Fall into Sin

This comes out very clearly in that beautiful passage, Hebrews 12:6–10:

> *For whom the Lord loveth he chasteneth, and scourgeth every son whom he receiveth. It is for chastening that ye endure; God dealeth with you as with sons; for what son is there whom his father chasteneth not? But if ye are without chastening, whereof all have been made partakers, then are ye bastards, and not sons. Furthermore, we had the fathers of our flesh to chasten us, and we gave them reverence: shall we not much rather be in subjection unto the Father of spirits, and live? For they indeed for a few days chastened us as seemed good to them; but he for our profit, that we may be partakers of his holiness.* (ASV)

Here we see that God's love manifests itself in chastening us and in sending us trial and pain and bereavement and sorrow. Many cannot see in their many and great afflictions any proof of God's love. It seems to them that God does not love them to allow them to suffer such awful and sometimes such appalling griefs and trials, but they who so think are very blind. Do we not chasten our own beloved children? Do we not do it because we love them and for their good? It would oftentimes be far easier for us not to do it. It would spare our feelings, for we suffer far more than they do when we punish them, if we are true parents. Some parents are so unloving and so self-centered that they allow their children to go unpunished in their folly and sin in order to spare their own feelings. But not so our heavenly Father. He really loves us, wisely loves us, and so chastens us for our highest good, and sometimes when our conduct makes it necessary, very severely chastises us, or as the Bible puts it, "*scourges*" us. Every wise man thanks God for His chastening love, even in its severest manifestations.

For twelve years or more God spared my wife and me and our family in our home life from serious sickness. We had gone through epidemics of many kinds unscathed. When threatened with croup, scarlet fever, typhoid fever, diphtheria, and other diseases, we had cried to God and He had given deliverance again and again. But a day came when God permitted diphtheria to enter our home, and a few short hours after the real character of the disease was discovered, to take away from us a beautiful child and to take her away when we thought all danger of death was past. It was a stunning blow, just twenty-four years ago this week, and March 17 never comes round without our thinking of it. For the first time, the family circle was broken. The body of our child had been carried from our happy home and laid away in the lonely cemetery. Why did God permit it? Because He loved us. We needed it.

The following Sunday night I spoke on Hebrews 12:6: "*For whom the Lord loveth he chasteneth, and scourgeth every son whom he receiveth.*" This chastisement, yes this scourging, led to deep heart searchings and discovery of failure and thereby led to confession of sin. It led also to new consecration and love for souls and devotion to God. It brought the answer to prayers that had been ascending to Him for years. It was one of the things that led to my leaving Chicago a few years later to enter upon a worldwide ministry. If God had not in His infinite wisdom and love taken our greatly beloved child, our rarely beautiful and gifted child from us, I think I would never have seen China, Japan, Australia, New Zealand, India, and the marvelous work of God in these countries, and the great work of God that followed in England, Ireland, Wales, Germany, and many other places. God's judgments are *"unsearchable," "his ways past finding out!"* (Romans 11:33), but they are always wise and loving, though we for the time cannot understand how. All of God's seemingly severe dealings with us came from the wise and wondrous love of God, and we both saw it and praised Him. There is no kinder manifestation of the love of God than His chastening us when we forget Him or wander from Him or become immersed in the world.

One beautiful spring day, years ago, a friend of mine in Ohio asked me to take a drive with him. We drove out into the country to a quiet cemetery. We entered and went to a remote corner of the cemetery and there found side by side three graves, one the grave of an adult, and the other two of children. They were the graves of that man's wife and his two little girls, all the family he had at the time in the world, with the exception of one little boy. We knelt beside the graves in prayer. As we drove back to town, that man said to me, "Brother Torrey, I pity the man whom God has not chastened."

What did he mean? He meant this: He had been a man of the world, an honorable, highly respected man, but a thoroughgoing worldling. Diphtheria came into *his* home. It took one of his little daughters. As she lay in her casket, the father knelt beside it and promised God that he would become a Christian. But when the first bitterness of the sorrow had passed, he forgot his vow. Again sickness and death entered his home. This time, the second daughter died. Beside her coffin, he renewed his vow, and kept it. He came to know the joy that every true Christian knows, to have the glorious hope for eternity that only the Christian has. He became, I think, take it all in all, the most active and efficient Christian in the community, and it all came from God's chastening love. He told me again and again that his favorite text of Scripture was,

"Whom the Lord loveth he chasteneth." Ah, friends, if some affliction has come upon you, see in it a token of God's love and learn the sweet lessons He would teach by this sorrow.

III. The Love of God Is Manifested by His Sympathizing with Us in All Our Afflictions

This comes out very clearly in a wonderful verse in the Old Testament, *"In all their affliction he was afflicted, and the angel of his presence saved them: in his love and in his pity he redeemed them; and he bare them, and carried them all the days of old"* (Isaiah 63:9). While God chastens us in His wise love to us, yes, even scourges us, when we forget Him and wander into sin and worldliness, nevertheless He deeply sympathizes with us in every sorrow, and trial, and heartache that our sin brings upon us. "In all our affliction he is afflicted." It may be His own hand that sends the affliction, as it was in the passage just read—we need the affliction, it does us good, so He sends it—but He suffers with us in it. *God is the great sympathizer:* "In all our affliction he is afflicted." In our own sorrow, we had many sympathizing human friends, and letters and telegrams of heartfelt sympathy poured in upon us. But no one sympathized with us as fully, as tenderly, as deeply, or as intelligently as God Himself. He saw what no human eye could see and entered into it all. And there were very many tender little ministries of His in those days of profound sorrow and many wondrous great ministries also. No human being will ever know what Mrs. Torrey and I passed through the night following the burial of our little child, and the next morning. The waters were deep. It seemed as if they would go over our heads, but One walked beside us. It was God. He suffered with us. He kept His Word: *"When thou passest through the waters, I will be with thee; and through the rivers, they shall not overflow thee: when thou walkest through the fire, thou shalt not be burned; neither shall the flame kindle upon thee"* (Isaiah 43:2).

Friends, some of you are in deep sorrow, some in sorrow of one kind and some in sorrow of an entirely different kind, but I want to tell you one and all that God sympathizes with you all in your sorrow, whatever it may be. It may seem to you that no one sympathizes with you, that no one even understands, that no one cares, and that may be true of men, but it is not true of God. He understands it all and enters into it all. "Our Father cares."

A woman came to see me at the hotel where I was stopping in Bendigo, Australia. She told me that an awful sorrow had come into her life, but that she could not tell it to any one there, for they all knew her. I was a stranger and would soon leave the place, and her burden was so heavy she felt that she must have the sympathy of someone, and so she had come to me. It was a terrible story that she told me. She was passing through one of the greatest sorrows that ever overtakes any true woman, and her heart was nearly crushed. When she had finished that sad story, she said to me, "I feel better now that there is someone who knows my sorrow and can sympathize with me." I said to her, "I do indeed sympathize with you. I am glad you came and told me the story that I might help you bear your burden. But," I added, "there is One who has known all about it from the beginning. God has known all about it and He has sympathized with you all the time." Oh, it is true. Not a sorrow, not a heartache, not a disappointment, not a calamity, not a grief, ever comes to us but our Heavenly Father knows it all, knows it in all its details, and sympathizes with us in all the suffering. He Himself suffers far more than we suffer.

IV. God's Love Is Manifested in His Never Forgetting Those Whom He Loves

In the fourth place, *God's love is manifested in His never forgetting those whom He loves*. This He Himself tells us in the wonderful words in Isaiah 49:15–16: *"Can a woman forget her sucking child, that she should not have compassion on the son of her womb? yea, they may forget, yet will not I forget thee. Behold, I have graven thee upon the palms of my hands; thy walls are continually before me."* God sometimes seems to forget, but He never does. We cry and no answer comes. The heavens seem to be as brass above our heads, but God has not forgotten. *He never forgets.* A mother may forget her child, though that is not likely, yet she may, but God has said, *"Yet will not I forget thee."* He has said furthermore, *"Behold, I have graven thee upon the palms of my hands."*

V. God's Love Is Manifested in His Forgiving Our Sins

Hezekiah cried unto the Lord: *"Behold, it was for my peace that I had great bitterness: but thou hast in love to my soul delivered it from the pit of corruption; for thou hast cast all my sins behind thy back"* (Isaiah 38:17 ASV). God stands ready in His love to pardon the sins of the vilest sinner. There are two things and only two that in His love He demands as a condition of that pardon. They are, first, that we forsake our sins; second, that we turn to Him in faith and surrender to His will. Listen to His own word: *"Let the wicked forsake his way, and the unrighteous man his thoughts; and let him return unto the LORD, and he will have mercy upon him; and to our God, for he will abundantly pardon"* (Isaiah 55:7). God will not pardon our sins if we hold on to them. There is a theory regarding God's love current in the world today that has no warrant in the Word of God: namely, that, because *"God is love"* He will pardon and save all men whether they repent and believe on Jesus Christ or not.

This theory is wholly and utterly unscriptural. To believe it, you must give up the Bible. But if you give up the Bible, you must give up your belief that *"God is love,"* for it is from the Bible and from the Bible alone that we learn that *"God is love."* There is absolutely no other proof that *"God is love"* than that the Bible says so. That is proof enough, for the Bible can be easily proven to be the Word of God. But if you give up the Bible and are logical, you must give up your belief that God is love, for when the Bible is gone, the belief that God is love has no foundation of any kind. But if you retain the Bible, you cannot believe that God will pardon and save all men whether they repent or not. The most illogical system in the world (except Unitarianism) is Universalism. It starts out with the Bible statement that *"God is love"* as its foundation stone. Then it goes to work to discredit the Bible by rejecting other plain statements in it, statements about hell, and the future state of those who reject Christ, and by doing that it undermines the authority of the Bible, and thus undermines the foundation of our faith that *"God is love."* In other words, it tries to build up a superstructure by undermining its foundation. Give up the Bible and there is no proof that *"God is love,"* and so Universalism goes by the board. Believe in the Bible, and you must believe in hell, and so Universalism goes by the board. Take either horn of the dilemma you please, and Universalism has absolutely no foundation. The very love of God, God's love to the righteous and His love to His Son Jesus Christ, demands that if men persist in sin and persist in the rejection of His Son Jesus Christ, that they be separated from the righteous and punished. *The love of God makes hell a necessity if men persist in sin.* And, if they persist eternally in sin, it makes eternal hell a necessity. And it is psychologically certain, as well as clearly revealed in the Bible, that if men persist in sin beyond a certain point they will persist in sin eternally.

But if the vilest sinner repents, God will pardon. He says so. He goes so far as to say in Isaiah 1:18: *"Come now, and let us reason together, saith Jehovah; though your sins be as scarlet, they shall be as white as snow; though they be red like crimson, they shall be as wool"* (ASV). A man once said to me, "My sins are too great for God to pardon."

I answered, "I do not wish you to think that your sins are any less than you now think they are. No doubt they are even greater than you think, but I want you to see that great as your sins are God's pardoning love is greater still." How often God proved this in the Bible. David's sin was great—it was monstrous—he was an adulterer and a murderer; yet God pardoned him. Manasseh's sin was exceeding great. He hated God and he hated God's people, and he made the streets of Jerusalem run with the blood of God's servants, yet God pardoned him. (See 2 Kings 24:3–4; see also 2 Chronicles 33:1–13.) Saul of Tarsus was a great sinner. He hated Jesus Christ, he persecuted the disciples of Jesus Christ and took part in their murder, and he was a bold blasphemer and compelled others to blaspheme; yet God pardoned him. So down through the centuries many of the vilest sinners this world has ever seen have repented, and God has pardoned them. There sit in this building tonight men and women who have gone down into the deepest depths of sin, but God has pardoned and saved them, and they sit here tonight rejoicing in His pardoning love, knowing that their every sin is blotted out, and furthermore, they have been transformed by the power of His grace.

VI. God's Love was Manifested in His Giving His only Begotten Son to Die for Us

God's love was manifested in His giving His only begotten Son to die in our place. As the Spirit of God puts it in John 3:16: *"For God so loved the world, that he gave his only begotten Son, that whosoever believeth in him should not perish, but have everlasting life."* And again we read in Romans 8:32: *"He spared not his own Son, but delivered him up for us all"*; and we read in 1 John 4:10: *"Herein is love, not that we loved God, but that he loved us, and sent his Son to be the propitiation for our sins."* Back in the prophetic vision of the Old Testament, seven hundred years before the Savior was born, we read: *"All we like sheep have gone astray; we have turned every one to his own way; and the* L*ORD hath laid on him the iniquity of us all"* (Isaiah 53:6). This manifestation of God's love is greatest of all. This manifestation of God's love is stupendous. It seems past believing, but we know it is true. God made the greatest sacrifice in His power for our good. He made the greatest sacrifice in the world's history, He *gave up* that which was dearest to Him, *His only Son.*

No earthly son was ever as dear to his father as Jesus Christ was dear to God. I have a son, an only son, and I love him, but my love for my boy is but the faintest adumbration of God's love to Jesus Christ. And yet God gave up that only begotten Son, that eternally beloved Son, for you and me. Gave Him up to die. To die an awful death, an appalling death. Gave Him up to be crushed by the weight of man's sin and guilt. And for what purpose did He give Him up? *"That whosoever believeth on him should not perish but have everlasting life."* God has done everything in His power to provide everlasting life for each one of us. If we do not have it, it is our own fault: God has exhausted the resources of infinite wisdom and infinite love and infinite power to provide everlasting life for you and me, and you and I can have it for the taking.

Such is the love of God, very inadequately described. But I wish to ask a question in closing. The question is this: *What are you going to do with that wondrous love of God tonight?* Our guilt never looks as black as when seen in the dazzling light of God's amazing love. To be a sinful man or woman seems bad enough, to despise and break God's holy and excellent laws seems bad enough, but the worst thing about men and women out of Christ, the most shocking thing about men and women out of Christ, the most horrible thing about men and women out of Christ, the most damnable and damning thing about men and women out of Christ is, that *they are trampling underfoot the love of God.* What would you think of a man who had a true and loving mother, a mother who had done everything for him, a mother who had made every sacrifice for him, a mother who had impoverished herself and imperiled and wasted her life for him, and then he despised that love, rejected that love, sneered at that love, denied that love, and sought to discredit that love? Would you not say that that man was a wretch? But no mother's love is as great and wonderful as the love of God to you and me. No mother ever made a sacrifice for her child as great as God has made for you and me. Now what will you do with that love tonight? Will you accept it or despise it? Will you put your trust in it or spurn it? Will you open your heart to it or spit upon it? What will you do with it?

Oh, men and women, are you rejecting Christ? Are you trampling underfoot the wondrous love of God revealed by giving His Son to die on Calvary's cross for you? If you are, what have you to say for yourselves? Oh, give up your awful treatment of this glorious Son of God, and accept Him now as your personal Savior, and surrender to Him as your Lord and Master, begin the confession of Him, a confession that most of you should have begun long, long ago, and go out from this place tonight to serve Him all the remainder of your days with all your strength.

3

THE MOST WONDERFUL SENTENCE EVER WRITTEN

"For God so loved the world, that he gave his only begotten Son, that whosoever believeth in him should not perish, but have everlasting life."
—John 3:16

My text is, "The most wonderful sentence that was ever written." Of course, that sentence is in the Bible. All the greatest sentences that were ever written are found in one book, God's Word, the Bible. The Bible is a book that abounds in illuminating, stirring, startling, marvelous, bewildering, amazing and life-transforming utterances, utterances with which there is absolutely nothing to compare in all the other literature of the world. But I am inclined to think that the one we are to consider tonight is the most remarkable of them all. I think that after we have given it careful thought, you will agree with me that this sentence is the most wonderful that was ever written.

You are all perfectly familiar with it. I doubt if there is a person in this audience who has not heard it again and again. Indeed, our very familiarity with it has blinded many of us to the wonderful character of it and the stupendous significance of it. But we are going to look at it steadily and closely, turning it around and around, as one would turn around and scrutinize a diamond of unusual purity, beauty, brilliance, and play of prismatic colors, until its beauty, its profundity, its glory, its sublimity, and its amazing significance are more fully seen and appreciated by us.

The sentence is found in John 3:16, *"For God so loved the world, that he gave his only begotten Son, that whosoever believeth in him should not perish, but have everlasting life."* There are whole volumes of incomparably precious truth packed into that one sentence. Indeed, many volumes have been devoted to the exposition of that one verse, but it is not exhausted yet and never will be. These marvelous words of God never become hackneyed, worn out, or wearisome. We are always beholding new beauty and new glory in them. When all the millions of volumes that men have written in many languages throughout the many centuries of literary history have become obsolete and are forgotten, that imperishable sentence shall shine out in its matchless beauty and peerless glory throughout the endless ages of eternity. Let me repeat it again, *"For God so loved the world, that he gave his only begotten Son, that whosoever believeth in him should not perish, but have everlasting life."* God Himself has used that statement to save thousands of souls, to lift men out of the sad, yes appalling ruin that sin had wrought into the glory of likeness to Himself. I trust that He may use it tonight to save many more.

The verse tells us five exceedingly important facts: First, God's attitude toward the world; second, God's attitude toward sin; third, God's attitude toward His Son; fourth, God's attitude toward all who believe in His Son; fifth, God's attitude toward all who refuse or neglect to believe in His Son.

I. God's Attitude Toward the World

What is God's attitude toward the world? *Love*. The sentence reads, "*God so **loved** the world.*" Love is the most wonderful thing in the world, and love is one of the most uncommon things in the world. There is in the world today much that is called "love," but most of that which is called love is not love at all. We speak oftentimes of a young man's "love" for a young woman, and all we mean by it is that this young man wishes to get that young woman for his own pleasure and gratification. That is not love at all; it oftentimes has not the slightest semblance of love. It is oftentimes utter selfishness, and not infrequently the vilest and most unbridled lust. It is not at all unlikely that if the young woman refuses to accept him as a husband or so-called "lover," he will shoot her down or seek to blast her reputation. And that hideous thing we call "love"! He "loved" her so much that he killed her. It is really as remote from love as anything possibly can be, as remote from love as hell is from heaven. It is the very lowest order of selfishness and the grossest beastliness. The week before last, when a lawyer here in this city shot his former wife in the back, when she was not looking, because she would not return to him and endure longer the outrages that he had inflicted upon her for years, was it love that prompted his amazingly cowardly, sneaking, cruel, ruffianly, devilish act? No! It was a passion that would have disgraced the lowest wild beast of the jungle.

We speak of one man's love for another. What do we usually mean? Only this, the two men are friendly because in many respects they are congenial and enjoy one another's society. But if one does some little thing that offends the other, the so-called love is turned into utter indifference or even into bitter hate. It was never "love." It was mere self-centered fondness.

All this is not love. What is love? *Love is the consuming, absorbing desire for and delight in another's highest good.* Real love is entirely unselfish. It loses sight utterly of self-interest and sets itself to seeking the interest of the person loved. This was God's attitude toward the world. He *loved* the world, really loved it.

He looked down upon this world, the whole mass of men living at any time upon it and that would live upon it in all times to come, and He loved them all. His whole being went out in infinite yearning to benefit and bless the world. Any cost to Himself would be disregarded, if it would bless the world to pay the cost. "*God so loved the world, that* ***he gave his only begotten Son.***" Oh, men and women, stand and wonder! Oh, angels, and archangels, cherubim and seraphim, stand and wonder! "*God* ***so*** *loved the world,* ***that he gave his only begotten Son.***"

Some men tell us that they cannot believe the Bible to be the Word of God because there are so many incredible statements in it. But that is the most incredible statement in the whole Book, and yet we know it is true. If I can believe that statement, I should not have any difficulty with any other statement in the whole Book, and I can believe that statement. I *do* believe that statement. I know that statement is true. I have put it to the test of personal experience and found it true. "*God so loved the world, that he gave his only begotten Son*"; that has been God's attitude toward the world from the beginning. That is God's attitude toward the world tonight.

God loves *the world*. There are men and women and children in this world whom you and I love, but God loves the whole world. There is not a man in it, not a woman in it, not a child in it whom God does not love. From the intellectually most rarely gifted and morally most saintly man and woman down to the most ignorant, naked African in the heart of the Dark Continent, and the morally most degraded and brutelike man or woman in the slums of a great city or in the jungles of some cannibal island, God loves each and every one. "*God so loved* ***the world.***"

There are hundreds and hundreds of people who gather in this church, about whom you care absolutely nothing. You never saw them before, and you will never see them again. If you were to read in your paper tomorrow morning, "John Jones, who was at the Church of the Open Door, as he was going home from the meeting, got in front of a Sixth Street car and was instantly killed," you would hardly give it a second thought. John Jones is nothing to you. But John Jones is something to God. God loves John Jones, and John Smith, and John Johnson, and every other man and woman and child. You may be a very lonely stranger in a great city's crowd. Perhaps you have been unfortunate and are penniless and friendless. Perhaps you have gone down into some black depth of sin and you say to yourself, "Not one person in this great crowd has the slightest interest in me," and that may be true. But there is One who has an interest in you. There is One who so loved you that He *"gave his only begotten Son"* to die for you, and that One is God. God loves the world and every one in it. God loves the world in the purest, deepest, and highest sense of that word "love." Yes, God loves you. "Who do you mean by *you?*" someone asks. I mean every man, woman, and child.

There is nothing about the world why God should love it. It is a sinful world. It is a selfish world. It is a corrupt world. The more I get to know the world of which I am a part, and the more I get to know myself, the more I am humbled. John was entirely right when he said, *"The whole world lieth in the evil one"* (1 John 5:19 ASV). I am an optimist, but I am not an optimist by painting a black world white. Look at the rich world. What a cruel thing it is. How it marches on, trampling down everyone that lies in its path to greater wealth. How are great fortunes usually built up? You know. I know. By the trampling of human hearts underfoot. But look at the poor world. It is nearly as cruel as the rich world. One day in Chicago, two men were working hard to make an honest living for themselves and families just four doors north of the church of which I was pastor. Four other poor men sneaked in and chopped their heads open with hatchets, and ran.

Why did they do it? Simply because they wanted the jobs of these two men. The two men struck down by the four heartless cowards were guilty of no crime and no wrong against the ones that cut them down. They did not belong to the union; that was all. If you wish to know the spirit of the rich world, look at some of the greedy, conscienceless Trusts. If you wish to know the spirit of the poor world, look at the present day methods of the Trades Unions. The spirit of both is essentially the same, greed for gold; money must be secured at any cost, even the cost of murder of others by the slow process of starvation on the part of the rich, or the rapid process of hatchet and bullet and dynamite on the part of the poor.

This is a cruel, selfish, bloodthirsty world. We saw what the world really is in the late war. But God loves it. God loves those four cowards who cut down their fellow laboring men. God loves those millionaires who, already having more than is for their own good or for the good of their families, are trying to increase their wealth by crowding competitors to the wall and their families to the poorhouse. God loves those moral monsters that made Europe flow with blood and gasp with poison gas. God loves the world. As I come to know more and more of the cruelty, the greed, the avarice, the selfishness, the falsehood, the villainy, the lust, the vileness, and beastliness there is in this world, in the social world, high and low, in the business world in all its departments, and in the political world, I sometimes almost wonder why God does not blot out this whole world as He did Sodom and Gomorrah of old.

Why does He not do it? I will tell you why. God *loves* the world. In spite of all its cruelty, in spite of all its greed, in spite of all its selfishness, in spite of all its lust, in spite of all its vileness in thought and word and deed, God loves the world. Is it not wonderful, is it not amazing, that a holy God should love a sinful world like this? But He does!

There is not a man whom God does not love. There is not a woman whom God does not love. There is not a thief whom God does not love. There is not a woman who has forgotten her modesty and her true womanhood that God does not love. There is not an adulterer whom God does not love, not a sinner, not an outcast, not a criminal of any kind whom God does not love. "*God so loved* ***the world.***"

Years ago, I said to a woman, in deep despair because of the depths of iniquity and infamy into which she had fallen, "God loves you." "Not me, Mr. Torrey. God doesn't love me. I have killed a man," she cried. "Yes, I know that, but God loves you." "No, not me. I have murdered innocent, unborn babes." "Yes, I know that, but God loves you." "Not me. My heart is as hard as a rock." "Yes, but God loves you." "Not me. I have prayed to the devil to take away all my convictions, and he has done it." "Yes, I know all that, but God loves you." Then I made that woman get down on her knees, and she came to believe in God's love to her, and she found a great peace. I saw her again last month when I was in Chicago. She came down to the platform to speak to me at the close of one of my meetings, with others who crowded around me. She said, "Do you know me?" I replied, "Of course, I know you," and called her by name. Her face was wreathed with smiles. "Oh," she said, "Mr. Torrey, I am still at the old work of winning others to Christ." Ah, some of you self-righteous skeptics hold up your hands in holy horror and disgust and say, "I don't want to believe in a God who welcomes sinners as vile as that." You miserable Pharisee, you old hypocrite, you are essentially as bad as she once was and infinitely worse than she now is. But God loves you, even you. God's attitude toward the whole wide world is love.

II. God's Attitude Toward Sin

Our text tells us, *God's attitude toward sin is* ***hate***. God loves the world with infinite love! God hates sin with infinite hate! How does our text show that? Listen. *"God* ***so*** *loved the world,* ***that he gave his only begotten Son,*** *that whosoever believeth in him should not perish, but have everlasting life."* How does that show that God hates sin? In this way: If God had not hated sin, He could have saved the world He loved without an atonement, without the atonement that cost Him so much, the death and agony of His only begotten Son, who died as an atoning sacrifice on the cross. But because God was holy and therefore hated sin, hated it with infinite hatred, His hatred of sin must manifest itself somehow, either in the punishment of the sinner, and the banishment of the sinner forever from Himself and from life, and from hope, or in some other way. But God's love would not permit the just punishment of the sinner. So God in the person of His Son took the penalty of sin upon Himself and thus saved the world He loved. "All we like sheep have gone astray; we have turned everyone to his own way; and Jehovah *hath made to strike on him* the iniquity of us all" (Isaiah 53:6, exactly translated from the Hebrew). In this way God made possible eternal life for every sinner who would accept the salvation that He Himself purchased for them by the atoning death of His only begotten Son.

The cross of Christ declares two things: first, God's infinite love of the world; second, God's infinite hatred of sin. Oh, wicked man, do not imagine that because God loves you, He will wink at your sin. Not for one moment. He hates your sin. He hates your greed. He hates your selfishness. He hates your cruelty. He hates your dishonesty. He hates your lying. He hates your drunkenness. He hates your impure imagination. He hates your moral uncleanness. He hates your beastliness. He hates every sin, great and small, of which you are guilty. The hatred of a true man for all falsehood, the hatred of honest men for all dishonesty, the hatred of a true, pure woman for the unspeakable vileness of the woman of the street and gutter, is nothing to the blazing wrath of God at your smallest sin. Nevertheless, God loves you.

III. God's Attitude Toward His Son

This wonderful verse also tells of God's attitude toward His Son. *"God so loved the world, that he gave his* ***only begotten Son."*** *God's attitude toward His Son, "his only begotten Son," is infinite love.* The Lord Jesus is the only Son of God. We become sons of God through our faith in Him, but He is the only Son of God by eternal and inherent right. He was the object of His Father's infinite love in the measureless ages before any one of the worlds was created; yes, before there was angel or archangel or any of the heavenly beings. Let me speak to you fathers. What is your attitude toward your son? How you love him. And if you have only one son, how intensely you love him. I have but one son. I have longed for more, but God in His wisdom has seen fit to give us but one son. How I love him! God only knows how I love him. But my love to my one son is nothing, nothing at all to God's love to His only begotten Son.

I sometimes think of my boy and imagine I know something of God's love for Jesus Christ, but it is only a little, a very little that I know. But though God thus loved His Son, God gave that Son whom He so infinitely loved, that Son who through all eternity had been the object of His delight. God gave that only begotten Son for the world, for you and for me. He gave Him to leave heaven and His own companionship to come down to earth to live a lonely stranger here. He gave Him to be spit upon and buffeted and "*despised and rejected of men*" (Isaiah 53:3). He gave Him to be crowned with thorns, and mocked at and derided. He gave Him to be dragged through the streets before a howling, yelling, jeering mob. He gave Him to be nailed *to the cross*. Yes, to a cross! And to hang there in misery, and pain, and agony, for hours, the object of the rude jests and jeers of the merciless mob. He gave Him to die of a "broken heart," a heart broken by the reproach of the men He loved (see Psalm 69:20), and by grief over man's sins that He had taken upon Himself. Yes, God gave Him, *his only begotten son,* thus to be separated from Himself, to suffer, and to die. Why? Because God loved you and me, and that was the only price that would purchase our salvation. And God paid that price, that awful price.

Oh, it is wonderful! I can think of only one other thing that is anywhere near as wonderful as the love of God for sinners. What is that? The way we treat that love. The way men treat it. The way some of you despise it. The way you reject it. The way you trample it underfoot. The way you even try to doubt it and disbelieve it and deny it and discredit it, and try to make yourself think that you have "intellectual difficulties about the Doctrine of the Atonement." Men, at least be honest. Your real difficulty is not intellectual. You want to save your pride, and excuse the enormity of your ingratitude. And to do that you do not hesitate at the gross sin of "*even denying the Lord that bought*" you, bought you by His atoning agony and death. (See 2 Peter 2:1.) Oh, be honest with the wondrous love of God, even if you are determined to spurn it. Your pretended "theological difficulties with the atonement" that Jesus Christ made upon the cross are simply your dishonest attempt to excuse your abominable ingratitude and damnable rejection of infinite love. Bear with me for talking thus plainly about your sin. I do it in love to you. You may not be willing to admit that tonight, but you will have to admit it in that day when you stand in the light of the Great White Throne where all lies and pretexts and deceptions and hypocrisies will be burned up.

IV. God's Attitude Toward Believers in Christ

What is God's attitude toward all who believe in Jesus Christ? It can be put in a few words. *God's attitude toward all believers in Jesus Christ is to give them eternal life. "God so loved the world, that he gave his only begotten Son,* ***that whosoever believeth in him should not perish, but have everlasting life."*** The death of Jesus Christ has opened a way of pardon for all who believe in Him, and made it possible for a Holy God to forgive sin and to give eternal life to the vilest sinner, if only he will believe on Jesus Christ. "*The wages of sin is death,*" and these wages must be paid, but Jesus Christ paid the price and so life and not death is possible for you and me. "*The free gift of God is eternal life in Christ Jesus our Lord*" (Romans 6:23 ASV). "*Whosoever*" believes on Jesus Christ, whom God gave to die for him, can have eternal life, yes, does have eternal life. Anyone can have eternal life. There is but one condition, just believe on Jesus Christ. You ought to do it anyhow, even if there were nothing to be gained by your believing on Him; you owe it to Jesus Christ to believe on Him. He is infinitely worthy of your faith.

But there *is* something to be gained by believing on Him, something of infinite worth: eternal life. Do you wish eternal life? You can have it. Anyone can have it, no matter what his past may have been. "*God so loved the world, that he gave his only begotten Son, that whosoever* ***believeth*** *in him should not perish, but have everlasting life.*" Oh, if I offered you great honor, it would be nothing compared with this. If I offered you enormous wealth, it would be nothing compared with this. If I offered you exemption from all sickness and pain, it would be nothing compared with this. Eternal life! That is what God offers. And God offers it to each one of you. Oh, how it makes the heart swell and throb with hope and joy and rapture. Eternal life!

V. God's Attitude Toward All Those who Will Not Believe in Christ

There is just one thing left to mention, and that is God's attitude toward all those who will not believe on Jesus Christ. *"For God so loved the world, that he gave his only begotten Son, that* ***whosoever believeth on him should not perish,*** *but have everlasting life." God's attitude toward those who will not believe on Jesus Christ, those who prefer sin and vanity and pride to the glorious Son of God, is simply this: God with great grief and reluctance withdraws from them the infinite gift He has purchased at so great cost, and which they will not accept.* ***God leaves them to perish.*** There is no hope for any man who rejects God's gift of eternal life, obtained by simply believing in His only begotten Son. God has exhausted all the possibilities of a saving love and power in Jesus Christ's atonement on the cross of Calvary. Reject Him, neglect to accept Him, and you must eternally perish.

God's attitude toward the world is infinite love. God's attitude toward sin is infinite hatred. God's attitude toward His Son is unutterable love, but He gave that Son up to die for you and me. God's attitude toward the believer is to give him eternal life, regardless of what his past has been. God's attitude toward those who will not believe is to leave them to the perdition they so madly choose. Men and women, what will you choose tonight, Life or Death? Some of you will decide that question in a few minutes, decide it for all eternity. God help you to decide it right.

One night in Minneapolis, years ago, I knelt in prayer beside a young woman who was having an awful struggle. A fearful battle was going on in her soul between the forces of light and the forces of darkness. She heard God calling her to accept His love, and to accept the eternal life that that love had purchased by the atoning death of His own Son. But she heard other voices too, voices of the world, and the voice of Satan himself, luring her to turn her back upon Jesus Christ and choose the world. It was awful to watch the battle, and my heart ached as I watched, and I kept crying to God that the Holy Spirit might gain the victory. Now and then I spoke to her. Finally I took out my watch and said, "This battle cannot last much longer. Continue to resist the Holy Spirit as you are resisting Him now, and you will seal your doom. I believe if you do not yield to God in the next ten minutes that you will never yield but will be lost forever." Then I prayed but said nothing more to her, but now and again looked at my watch. The fight went on. Which way would she decide! Before the ten minutes were up, she yielded to God.

There is a similar battle going on in the hearts of some who are reading these words. Some of you have been brought to realize the wondrous love of God for you as you have never realized it before. Some of you have been brought to see that eternal life is possible for you tonight if you will only choose Christ. But the power of the world and of sin and of Satan is strong upon you still, and the world, and sin, and above all Satan, will not let you go without making a mighty effort to keep you in his power, to blind you, and to forever destroy your soul. Oh, men and women out of Christ, each and every one of you look, look, look! Look once more at the cross of Christ. See Him hanging there in awful agony, paying the penalty of your sin, and as you look, listen once more to the precious words of the most wonderful sentence that was ever written, "*God so loved the world, that he gave his only begotten Son, that whosoever believeth in him should not perish, but have everlasting life.*" What will you do with that love tonight? Will you yield to it and believe on the Savior and obtain eternal life? Or will you trample that wondrous love of God under foot, and say again tonight, as you have often said before, "I will not accept Christ," and go out to perish, perish eternally?

One night, many years ago, I was preaching the first sermon I ever preached in the city of Chicago. (It was some years before I went there to live.) I was at the first International Convention of Christian Workers. The morning the Convention opened, I entered a little late, and the Nominating Committee was just bringing in its report. To my amazement, I heard them announce my name as nominated for Chairman of the Convention and President of the International Christian Workers' Association. I was not yet thirty years old, and there were many workers there who knew far more about aggressive methods of Christian work than I had ever learned.

However, there was nothing to do but to accept the position, and during the days of that wonderful Convention, I occupied the Chairman's seat. The Convention was held in the old First Methodist Church, in the heart of the city, at the corner of Washington and Clark Streets. When Sunday came, of course the church held its own services, but I was invited to preach at the evening service. There had been much prayer and the Spirit of God was present in great power, and when I gave out the invitation, many arose to say that they would accept Jesus Christ as their Savior then and there, and then came down to the altar. Among those who had arisen I noticed a beautifully dressed lady near the front, an intelligent looking woman, but I noticed also that she did not come to the altar with the others. While the altar service was in progress, I stepped down and urged her to come to the front, but she refused.

On Monday night, at the regular session of the Convention, I saw her come in and take a seat just a few rows from the back of the building. When the meeting was drawing to a close, I called Mayor Howland, of Toronto (who was vice president of the convention), to the chair and slipped down to the back of the church, in order that I might speak with this lady before she got out of the building.

The moment the benediction was pronounced, I hastened to her side and asked if she would remain a few moments. As the others passed out, she sat down, and I took a seat beside her and commenced to urge upon her an immediate and wholehearted acceptance of Jesus Christ.

"Let me tell you my story," she replied. "I have attended a Sunday school in this city ever since I was a little girl. I scarcely missed a Sunday." (She told me what Sunday school it was; one of the aristocratic Sunday schools on the North Side.) "But," she continued, "though I have been going to Sunday school all these years, do you know that you are the first person in all my life that ever spoke to me personally about my accepting Christ?" Then she went on to tell me the story of her life. She was unusually well educated, occupying a high position of responsibility, but the story that she told me of her career was so shameless that I was amazed that a woman of sense, to say nothing of character, would dream of telling such a story to a man. Then she hurried on and told me how she had passed the preceding Easter Sunday. It was a story I could not repeat. Having finished, she said, with a mocking laugh, "Funny way to spend Easter, wasn't it?"

I was astounded and shocked. I did not attempt to say anything in reply; I did not wish to. I simply opened my Bible to John 3:16, handed it to her and asked her to read. It was a diamond print Bible, and she had to hold it close to her face to see the words. She began to read with a smile on her lips, *"For God so loved the world"* (the smile vanished, but she read on) *"that he gave his only begotten Son."* She choked and broke down. The tears literally poured from her eyes on the page of the Bible and on the beautiful silk robe she wore. The love of God had conquered that sinful, hardened, trifling, seemingly shameless heart. Oh! Friend, I earnestly desire that that love might break your heart, break down your hardness, and unbelief, and worldliness, and resistance to God and His love.

See the Lord Jesus hanging on yonder cross in unutterable agony, in indescribable pain, His heart breaking for you, breaking for your sins, and hear again this most wonderful sentence that was ever written, *"For God so loved the world, that he gave his only begotten Son, that whosoever believeth in him should not perish, but have everlasting life."*

4

THE ONLY GOSPEL THAT HAS SAVING POWER

"For I am not ashamed of the gospel of Christ: for it is the power of God unto salvation to every one that believeth; to the Jew first, and also to the Greek."
—Romans 1:16

"But though we, or an angel from heaven, should preach unto you any gospel other than that which we preached unto you, let him be anathema. As we have said before, so say I now again, If any man preacheth unto you another gospel from other than that which ye received, let him be anathema."
—Galatians 1:8–9 (ASV)

We hear much in these days about various gospels. Some extol the "gospel of social service," others talk of the "gospel of the universal fatherhood of God and the universal brotherhood of man," the "gospel of work," and others of various other gospels. But there is but one real gospel, only one gospel that in actual fact has saving power. That gospel is "the gospel of Christ," the gospel that Paul preached, and of which he said that if any man, or even an angel from heaven, were to preach any other gospel, he would be accursed of God. All these other gospels have one fatal fault: they don't save. These other gospels may sound well. They may be described with entrancing rhetoric. They may be preached with great eloquence, with marvelous beauty of diction, with charming figures of speech. They may seem exceedingly alluring, *but they don't save.* For all their pretenses and prettiness, instead of saving, they darken, debase, and damn. They do not enlighten, elevate, and save.

I. Man's Need of Salvation

What man needs is salvation, not mere social uplifting or mere moral improvement, not mere intellectual enlightenment. Man is lost. Every man is lost until he is definitely saved. The only thing that will save him is the gospel that Paul preached.

1. *Every man needs salvation from the guilt of sin.* Every man and woman on this earth is a sinner. Every man and woman on this earth has been a great sinner. Every man and woman on this earth has broken the first and greatest of God's commandments, namely, *"Thou shalt love the Lord thy God with all thy heart, and with all thy soul, and with all thy mind"* (Matthew 22:37–38). Every one of us, therefore, is a guilty sinner in the sight of a Holy God, and we need salvation from the guilt of sin. That is the first need, the great need, the crying need, the fundamental need of every one of us.

2. But *every man also needs salvation from the power of sin.* Sin has a hold upon every one of us, a mastery over every one of us, that we cannot overcome in our own strength. We must find a deliverer from the power of sin. The one universal need is the need of salvation, the need of salvation from the guilt and power of sin.

3. *The gospel has power to save.* As our text puts it, "*the gospel is the power of God unto salvation to everyone that believeth: to the Jew first, and also to the Greek,*" and no other religion of philosophy has power to save. Nothing else in the entire world has power to save from the guilt and power of sin.

II. What Is the Gospel?

The word "*gospel*" means, as I presume you all know, "good news" or "glad tidings." What is the good news, or the glad tidings, that has saving power in it? Paul himself told us what this gospel was that he preached, and of which he said, "*It is the power of God unto salvation to every one that believeth.*" We are not left to speculate about that, for Paul himself defined in the simplest and most easily understood terms exactly what the gospel was that he preached, the gospel that had saving power, and the only gospel that has saving power. You will find Paul's full, and at the same time very plain, description of the gospel that he preached in 1 Corinthians 15:1–4:

> *Now I make known unto you brethren, the gospel which I preached unto you, which also ye received, wherein also ye stand,* ***by which also we are saved****, if ye hold fast the word which I preached unto you, except ye believed in vain," and now comes the description of the gospel, "For I delivered unto you first of all that which I also received:* ***that Christ died for our sins*** *according to the scriptures; and* ***that he was buried;*** *and* ***that he hath been raised*** *on the third day according to the scriptures.* (ASV)

1. You notice first of all in regard to this gospel that Paul preached, that *the good news* is *facts,* not theories, not speculations, not guesses, but solid, substantial, established, unmistakable,

inescapable, absolutely sure facts. I am glad of that. Most of the gospels one hears nowadays are mere theories. The gospel of Christ is facts.

2. There are three facts that constitute the good news:

(A.) First, *"that Christ died for our sins."* That certainly is good news. You and I are sinners. Every one of us has sinned. If anyone here tonight seeks to deny that he is a sinner, his denial that he is a sinner does not make him any less a sinner. Indeed, it makes him all the more a sinner; for it makes him a liar, as well as a sinner in other respects. As we read in 1 John 1:8, 10, *"If we say that we have no sin, we deceive ourselves, and the truth is not in us....If we say that we have not sinned, we make him* [God] *a liar, and his word is not in us."* So, by the denial of our sin, we do not make ourselves any less sinners, but we prove ourselves to be liars and make ourselves guilty of the enormous sin of making God a liar. That is what every Christian Scientist does. He makes God a liar. And that is what everyone else who denies that he is a sinner does. He makes God a liar. God says that we are sinners, and when we deny the fact, we give the lie to God. Every man, therefore, who denies that he is a great sinner is a liar, and all liars, unless they repent, are bound for the eternal fire. God says in Revelation 21:8, *"The fearful, and the unbelieving, and the abominable, and murderers, and fornicators, and sorcerers, and idolaters,* ***and all liars****, their part shall be in the lake that burneth with fire and brimstone; which is the second death"* (ASV).

Not only are we sinners, but God is holy, infinitely holy, and cannot tolerate sin. God is *"of purer eyes than to behold evil,"* and He can *"not look on iniquity"* (Habakkuk 1:3), and someday you and I must meet Him. We must either meet Him bearing our sin, with all our sin upon us, or else we must find someone else to bear our sin for us. If we were to meet this Holy God with our sin upon us, then must we be forever banished from His presence, *"be punished with everlasting destruction from the presence of the Lord, and from the glory of his power"* (2 Thessalonians 1:9). But the gospel tells us that someone else has borne our sin in our place. It tells us that a competent sin-bearer has been found. It tells us that *"Christ died for our sins"* (1 Corinthians 15:3), that the Lord "Jesus paid our debt, all the debt we owe," that though "sin had left a crimson stain," "He washed it white as snow." Even Isaiah, seven hundred years before Christ, got a glimpse of this wonderful truth of the gospel. Speaking in the Holy Spirit, he said, *"All we like sheep have gone astray; we have turned every one to his own way; and the LORD hath laid on him the iniquity of us all"* (Isaiah 53:6). So if we accept the Lord Jesus who died for our sins as our substitute Savior, then no matter how long we have sinned, no matter how greatly we have sinned, we can meet God with absolutely no sin upon us, for God Himself has put it upon Another. So the Lord Jesus, by His death, saves us completely from all the guilt of sin.

(B.) The second fact that goes to make up the gospel is that *the Lord Jesus "was buried."* At first sight, it is not clear how this is "good news," but it is good news; for *the fact of His burial shows the reality of His death and the actuality and literalness of His resurrection.* The burial of Jesus Christ shows that the death of Jesus Christ was no sham death, no mere "illusion." It was not merely "mortal thought," as the Christian Scientists would have us believe. It was a *real death,* and therefore it was a *real atonement.* All that Christian Science and various other false systems offer us is a *sham atonement* for *imaginary sin,* and thus they offer us only a *sham salvation.* The gospel of Christ, the gospel that God makes known, the gospel that Paul preached, the gospel of a Savior who not only died, but was buried, offers us a *real atonement for sins* that we know are *very real* and *very great* and therefore it offers us *a real salvation* from the guilt of sin. This true gospel says to the vilest sinner in the world, There is perfect pardon and justification for you, for the Son of God really died, He was really buried, and there is therefore a real and perfect salvation for you from all your guilt: "*The blood of Jesus his Son cleanseth us from all sin*" (1 John 1:7).

(C.) The third fact in the good news is that *Jesus Christ rose again*, or as Paul put it in his description of the gospel in 1 Corinthians 15:4, "*He hath been raised on the third day according to the scriptures*" (ASV). That is certainly good news. In fact, it is great news. It is good news for many reasons, but especially good news from the standpoint of salvation, because it shows that Jesus Christ can not only save from all the guilt of sin by His atoning death, but that He can also save from all the power of sin by His resurrection power. As it is put in that wonderful verse in Hebrews, "*Wherefore also he is able to save to the uttermost them that draw near unto God through him, seeing he ever liveth to make intercession for them*" (Hebrews 7:25 ASV). We do not need salvation only from the guilt of sin, but we need just as much salvation from the power of sin. Supposing I were a great sinner and, through faith in Christ crucified, were to find salvation from all my guilt, and find perfect peace of conscience, and were to go out of here tonight very happy in the thought that all my sins were blotted out. Then suppose that tomorrow the same old temptations that have overcome me in the past—for example, the appetite for drink, or some form of lust or impurity, or an appetite for drugs, or an ungovernable temper—were to confront me, and I had no power to resist the temptation, and down I go. How much would such a salvation be worth? But Jesus Christ not only died and was buried, He rose again, and tonight He lives and He has all power in heaven and on earth and so He can save me from my appetite for drink, or from the power of any evil desire, or from my temper, or whatever my sin may be; and however weak I may be, I can begin here and now to live a clean and victorious life.

I have, I believe, related before the following incident of a man who once called upon me in Chicago. This man sought a private interview, and when we had taken our seats alone in Mr. Moody's office, the man said, "I want to tell you my story." He went on as follows: "I am a Scotchman. When I was a child of seven over in Scotland, I began to read the Bible through. One day I came to a passage in Deuteronomy that told me that if I should keep the law of God a hundred years and then broke it at one point after having kept it a hundred years, I would be under the curse of the broken law of God. Was that right?" "Yes," I replied. "The Bible doesn't put it in just that way, but the Bible does say, '*Cursed is every one that continueth not in all things which are written in the book of the law to do them*' (Galatians 3:10)." "That's the passage," he said, "that I found, and I knew that I had already broken the law of God, and therefore I knew that I was under the curse of the broken law. Though I was only seven years of age, I was in deep distress. Night after night, I went to bed and wept myself to sleep, thinking how I was under the curse of the broken law of God. But I went on reading my Bible, and the next year when I was eight years old I came to John 3:16, '*For God so loved the world, that he gave his only begotten Son, that whosoever believeth in him should not perish, but have everlasting life,*' and all my burden rolled away. Was I converted?" "Well," I replied, "that sounds like a good, evangelical conversion."

"Let me tell you the rest of my story," he continued. "I grew up to manhood. I came to America. I came out here to Chicago. I found work down in the stockyards. I am living down in the stockyards. Now, the stockyards, as you know, are a hard place, and I got to drinking and every little while, I go off on a drunk. What I have come to ask you is if there is any way in which I can get victory over the drink?" "You have come just to the right place," I replied. "I can answer your question. There *is* a way in which you can get victory over the drink. You have only believed half the gospel, and therefore you have only got half a salvation." I said, "Let me show you the whole gospel," and I opened to the fifteenth chapter of First Corinthians and read, "'*Moreover, brethren, I declare unto you the gospel which I preached unto you, which also ye have received and wherein ye stand; by which also ye are saved, if ye keep in memory what I have preached unto you, unless ye believed in vain, for I delivered unto you first of all that which I also received, how that Christ died for our sins according to the scriptures; and that he was buried, and that he rose again the third day according to the scriptures'* (verses 1–4).

"Now," I went on, "You have believed the first part of this gospel, that Christ died and was buried, and through believing that you have found pardon and peace." "Yes." "But," I continued, "that is only half the gospel. There is another half to it, and that is *that He rose again.* Do you believe that?" "I believe everything in the Bible," he replied. Again I asked, "Do you believe that Jesus rose again the third day?" "Yes, I do." "Very well, then, if He rose the third day, then He has all power in heaven and on earth." "Yes." "And He has power to keep you from the power of the drink, and from the power of sin. Do you believe that?" Yes," he said, "I do." "Will you trust Him to do it?" "I will," he replied. "Let us kneel down and tell God so," I said. We knelt side by side. I prayed first and then he prayed. These were about the words he uttered. "O God, I have been believing half the gospel, and I have had half a salvation. I have believed that part of the gospel that told me that Christ died for my sins according to the Scriptures and through believing that I have found pardon and peace; but now I have come to believe the other half of the gospel, that Christ not only died, but that He rose again and that He has all power in heaven and on earth and that He has power to keep me from the power of the drink."

Then he changed his mode of address and commenced speaking directly to Jesus Christ. "Lord Jesus," he said, "I believe that You are risen from the dead, and I believe that You have all power in heaven and on earth. I believe that You have power to save me from the drink. O Lord Jesus, save me from the power of drink right now. I ask it in Your own name. Amen." As he still knelt there, his head bowed in prayer, I said, "Did you really trust Him to do it?" He replied, "I did." He rose, I gave him some instruction as to how to make a success of this life upon which he had entered, he left the office, and I didn't hear from him for some weeks. Then I received a brief letter, but the letter was very much to the point. It ran this way: "Dear Mr. Torrey, I am so glad I came to see you. *It works.*"

Yes, thank God, it *does* work. It works with anyone who really believes it. The gospel of a Savior who died and was buried and rose again has power to save from the guilt of sin and it also has power to save from the power of sin. It has power *"to save* ***to the uttermost****"* those who come to God through Jesus Christ. And it is the only gospel that can do it. The gospel of Christian Science, with a sham death and a sham resurrection, cannot do it. The Gospel of New Thought cannot do it. The gospel of Theosophy cannot do it. The gospel of Social Service, of which we are hearing so much in our day, cannot do it. No gospel but the gospel of Jesus Christ, the gospel of a Savior who really died, who was really buried, and who really rose again, can do it. A short while ago, a well-known pastor in Los Angeles announced that he was going to preach a gospel "without an atonement of blood." Well, if he does, he will preach a gospel that cannot save, he will preach a gospel that will send men to hell and not a gospel that will ever fit men for heaven. And anyone who preaches a gospel that Christ died, but not a gospel that He rose again, will preach a gospel that will not save from the power of sin. But the gospel contained in this blessed Book of God, the gospel that Jesus both died and rose again, will save. It will save from both the guilt and the power of sin, it will *"save to the uttermost."*

III. Whom the Gospel Saves

The gospel does not save everybody. This gospel has been proclaimed for more than eighteen hundred years, but it has not saved everybody yet, and it never will. There are many in these days who are saying the gospel is a failure because the great majority of men and women are not saved. They say, "Christianity is a failure, because after eighteen centuries our governments are not Christian, and wars and other damnable things are still possible." But herein lies their mistake: God never intended the gospel to save everybody. He never gave it to save everybody. He never expected it to save everybody. He gave it to save those who would believe it and those only. It is not Christianity that has failed, but man that has failed, by rejecting this glorious gospel. The gospel has not failed because it has not saved everybody any more than a perfectly good medicine that will cure anybody who takes it fails where it doesn't cure those who don't take it. God has told us plainly from the beginning just who the gospel would save. Who does it save? Listen: *"The gospel...is the power of God unto salvation to* ***every one that believeth.****"* This tells us whom the gospel saves.

1. First of all, *it saves those who believe.* Not those who hear, but those who believe. The gospel does not save everyone who hears it. Millions of men have heard the gospel all through their lives and died in their sins and gone to hell. There are many who fancy that merely hearing the gospel or living in a Christian land makes them Christians. One night I approached a very intelligent looking man in Duluth, Minnesota. I said to him, "Are you a Christian?" He replied, "Certainly; do you think I am a Mohammedan?" He thought that simply because he was born and brought up in a Christian land and heard the gospel, that made him a Christian; but it does not. It is *believing* the gospel, not merely hearing the gospel, that saves. It is believing the gospel and not merely hearing it that makes one a Christian. The gospel does not even save the one who merely admires it. A man may have a great admiration for the gospel, for the profound philosophy of the Bible, and yet be an utterly unsaved man. *The gospel saves the one who believes it and him alone.* The one who believes what? *The gospel.* Really believes it,

believes it with the heart. The one who has that kind of faith that leads to action, the faith that:

(A.) leads you to accept Christ as your atoning Savior and to trust God to forgive you simply because Jesus Christ died in your place;

(B.) the faith that leads you to accept Christ as your risen Savior and to trust Him to deliver you from the power of sin;

(C.) the faith that leads you, having accepted Him, to show the reality of your faith by an open confession of Him before the world, as it is written, *"If thou shalt* ***confess with thy mouth Jesus as Lord****, and shalt* ***believe in thy heart*** *that God raised him from the dead, thou shalt be saved: for with the heart man believeth unto righteousness; and* ***with the mouth confession is made unto salvation****"* (Romans 10:9–10).

2. But it not only saves those who believe. It saves *"**every one** that believeth."* As it is put in our text, *"The gospel...is the power of God unto salvation to* ***every one that believeth****."* There is not a man or woman in this room tonight whom the gospel cannot save. There is not a man or woman in the world so sunken in sin, so lost to all that is good and true and pure, that the gospel cannot save, *if they will only believe.* There is not a man or woman so utterly weak and helpless in sin that the gospel will not save them *if they believe it.* Why then is there a man or woman in the world who is not saved? Why is there a man or woman in the world who is not saved from the guilt and power of sin? *Simply because you will not believe.* Let me illustrate. Here is a great Mogul engine on the track. It is coaled and has water in the boiler. There is fire underneath the boiler, and the steam is up. There is a full head of steam. There is power in that locomotive to draw a heavily loaded freight train up the steepest grade, and now that locomotive backs down to the train, and now the engineer reverses the lever and the locomotive starts up the grade, but not a car moves. Why not? Was it because

there was not power in the locomotive to draw the train? No, there was plenty of power for that. What was the trouble? The brakeman had not put in the coupling pin. And now the locomotive backs down again and backs up to the train of cars. The brakeman goes in between the tender of the locomotive and the train, and drops in a little coupling pin, and now the engineer reverses the lever and the locomotive starts up the track again, and this time the train moves up the grade. Just so, the gospel has the power to save, *if you couple on.* The gospel locomotive stands on the track. There is in that locomotive power to carry the train most heavily loaded with sin up the track. Steam is up. It is starting up the grade to glory. It can pull you, no matter how heavily weighted you are with tons of sin, up the grade to glory. Fall in line. Couple on. Faith is the coupling pin. Just believe the gospel. It rests with every man and woman here tonight to say whether you will be saved or not saved right now from the guilt and power of sin. It all turns upon whether you will or will not believe the gospel. *"For I am not ashamed of the gospel, for it is the power of God unto salvation to* ***every one that believeth.****"*

5

THE GREAT ATTRACTION: THE UPLIFTED CHRIST

"And I, if I be lifted up from the earth, will draw all men unto myself."
—John 12:32 (ASV)

In a recent advertisement of a Sunday evening service in one of our American cities, it was stated that there would be three attractions: a high-class movie show, a popular gospel pianist and his wife, and an aria from the opera *Madame Butterfly* rendered by a well-known prima donna. It is somewhat startling when an unusually gifted and popular preacher, or his advertising committee, thinks of the gospel of the Son of God as having so lost its power to draw that it must be bolstered up by putting on a selection from a very questionable opera, rendered by a professional opera singer, as an additional attraction to help out our once crucified and now glorified Savior and Lord.

This advertisement set me to thinking as to what really was the great attraction to men in this day as well as in former days?

At once, there came to my mind the words of our text containing God's answer to this question: *"**And I**, if I be **lifted up from the earth, will draw** all men unto myself."* There is nothing else that draws like the uplifted Christ. Movies may get a crowd of empty-headed and empty-hearted young men and maidens, and even middle-aged folks without brains or moral earnestness, for a time, but nothing really draws and holds the men and women who are worthwhile like Jesus Christ lifted up. Nineteen centuries of Christian history prove the drawing power of Jesus when He is properly presented to men. I have seen some wonderful verifications of the assertion of our text as to the marvelous drawing power of the uplifted Christ.

In London, for two continuous months, six afternoons and evenings each week, I saw the great Royal Albert Hall filled and even jammed, and sometimes as many turned away as got in, though it would seat 10,000 people by actual count and stand 2,000 more in the dome. On the opening night of these meetings, a leading reporter of the city of London came to me before the service began and said, "You have taken this building for two consecutive months?"

"Yes," I answered.

"And you expect to fill it every day?"

"Yes."

"Why," he said, "no one has ever attempted to hold two weeks' consecutive meetings here of any kind. Gladstone himself could not fill it for two weeks. And you really expect to fill it for two months?"

I replied, "Come and see."

He came and he saw.

On the last night, when the place was jammed to its utmost capacity and thousands outside clamored for admission, he came to me again and I said, "Has it been filled?" He smiled and said, "It has." But what filled it? No show on earth could have filled it once a day for many consecutive days. The preacher was no remarkable orator. He had no gift of wit and humor, and would not have exercised it if he had. The newspapers constantly called attention to the fact that he was no orator, but the crowds came and came and came; rainy days and fine days, they crowded in or stood outside, oftentimes in a downpour of rain, in the vain hope of getting in. *What drew them?* The uplifted Christ preached and sung in the power of the Holy Spirit, given in answer to the daily prayers of 40,000 people scattered throughout the earth.

In Liverpool, the Tournament Hall, that was said to seat 20,000 people, and that by actual count seated 12,500 comfortably, located in a very out-of-the-way part of the city, several blocks from the nearest streetcar line, and perhaps half a mile from all the regular streetcar lines, was filled night after night for three months, and on the last night they crowded 15,000 people into the building at seven o'clock, and then emptied it, and crowded another 15,000 in who had been patiently waiting outside; 30,000 people drawn in a single night!

By what? By whom? Not by the preacher, not by the singer, but by Him who had said nearly nineteen hundred years before, *"And I, if I be lifted up from the earth, will draw all men unto myself."*

I. The Exact Meaning of the Text

Let us now look at the exact meaning of the text.

1. First, *notice the speaker, and the circumstances under which He spoke.* The Speaker was our Lord Jesus. Not the Christ of men's imaginings, but the Christ of reality, the Christ of actual historic fact. Not the Christ of Mary Baker Eddy's maudlin fancy, or of Madam Besant's mystical imaginings, but the Christ of actuality,

who lived here among men and was seen, heard and handled by men, and who was soon to die a real death to save real sinners from a real hell to a real heaven.

The circumstances were these. Certain Greeks among those who went up to worship at the Jewish feast came to one of the apostles, Philip, and said, *"We would see Jesus"* (John 12:21). And Philip went to Andrew and told Andrew what these Greeks said. Andrew and Philip together came and told Jesus. In the heart-cry of these Greeks, *"We would see Jesus,"* our Lord recognized the yearning of the universal heart, the heart of Greek, as well as Jew, for a satisfying Savior. The Greeks had their philosophers and sages, their would-be satisfiers and saviors, the greatest the world has ever known: Socrates, Aristotle, Plato, Epictetus, Epimenides, and many others, but they did not save, and they did not satisfy, and the Greeks cried, *"We would see Jesus"*; and in their eager coming, Jesus foresaw the millions of all nations who would flock to Him when He had been crucified as the universal Savior, meeting all the needs of all mankind, and so He cried, *"And I, if I be lifted up from the earth, will draw all men unto myself."*

2. Second, *notice the words, "If I be lifted up."* To what does Jesus refer? The next verse answers the question. *"This he said, **signifying by what manner of death he should die**"* (verse 33 ASV). Jesus referred to His lifting up on the cross, to die as an atoning Savior for all mankind. This verse is often quoted as if it meant that, if we lifted up Christ in our preaching, He would draw men. That is true, and it is a crying shame that we do not hold just Him up more in our preaching, and we would draw far more people if we did; but that is not our Lord's meaning. The lifting up clearly referred not to His not being lifted up in our preaching, but to being His lifted up by His enemies on the cross, to expose Him to awful shame and to an agonizing death. It is Christ crucified who draws. It is Christ crucified who meets the deepest needs of the heart of all mankind. It is an atoning Savior—a Savior who atones for the

sins of men by His death, and thus saves from the holy wrath of an infinitely holy God—who meets the needs of men, and thus draws all men, for all men are sinners. Preach any Christ but a crucified Christ, and you will not draw men for long. Preach any gospel but a gospel of atoning blood, and it will not draw for long.

Unitarianism does not draw men. Unitarian churches are born only to die. Their corpses strew New England today. Many of their ministers have been intellectually among the most brilliant our country has ever known, but their churches even under scholarly and brilliant ministers die, die, die. Why? Because Unitarianism presents a gospel without *atoning blood*, and Jesus has said and history has proven it true, *"And I,* ***if I be lifted up from the earth,*** *will draw all men unto myself."* "Christian Science," strangely so-called, for as has been often truly said, "it is neither Christian nor scientific," draws crowds of men and women of a certain type, men and women who have or imagine that they have physical ailments, and who will follow anything no matter how absurd, that promises them a little surcease from their real or imagined pains. It also draws crowds who wish to fancy that they have some religion without paying the price of true religion, genuine love, real self-sacrifice, and costly sympathy. But Christian Science does not draw *all* men; that is, all kinds and conditions and ranks of men. In fact, for the most part it does not draw men at all, but women, and the alleged men it draws see an easy way to make a living by preying upon the credulity of luckless females. No, a bloodless gospel, a gospel with a Christ but not a Christ lifted up on a cross, does not meet the universal needs of men, and so does not draw all men.

Congregationalism of late years has been sadly tinctured with Unitarianism. In spite of the fact that it has been an eyewitness to Unitarianism's steady decay and death, Congregationalism has largely dropped the atoning blood out of its theology, and consequently it is rapidly going to the wall. Its once great Andover

Seminary, still great in the size of its endowment that was given for the teaching of Bible Orthodoxy, but which the conscienceless teachers of a bloodless theology have deliberately taken for the exploitation of their *"damnable heresies"* (2 Peter 2:1), and which is still great in the number of its professors, graduated at their annual graduating exercises last spring just three men, one a Japanese, one a Hindu, and one an American. A theology without a crucified Savior, without the atoning blood, won't draw. It does not meet the need. No, no, the words of our Lord are still true, *"And I, **if I be lifted up from the earth**, will draw all men unto myself."*

3. *Note,* third, *the words "draw all men."* Does *"all men"* mean all individuals or men of all races? Did Jesus mean that every man and woman who lived on this earth would be drawn to Him, or did He mean that men of all races would be drawn to Him? The context answers the question. The Greeks, as we have seen, came to one of the apostles, Philip, and said, *"We would see Jesus."* Philip had gone and told Andrew, and Andrew and Philip had gone and told Jesus. Our Lord's ministry during His earthly life was to Jews only, and in the coming of these Greeks so soon before His death, our Lord saw the presage of the coming days when by His death on the cross, the barrier between Jews and Gentiles would be broken down and all nations would have their opportunity equally with the Jews, when by His atoning death on the cross men of all nations would be drawn to Him. He did not say that He would draw every individual, but that all races of men, Greeks as well as Jews, Romans, Scythians, French, English, Germans, Japanese, Americans, and men of all nations. He is a universal Savior, and true Christianity is a universal religion. Mohammedanism, Buddhism, Confucianism, and all other religions but Christianity are religions of a restricted application. Christianity, with a crucified Christ as its center, is a universal religion and meets the needs of all mankind. It meets the needs of the European as well as the needs of the Asian, the needs of the Occident as well as the needs

of the Orient, the needs of the American Indian and the needs of the African; and so our Lord said, *"And I, if I be lifted up from the earth, will draw all men unto myself."*

No race has ever been found anywhere on this earth to which the gospel did not appeal and whose deepest need the crucified Christ did not meet. Many years ago, when Charles Darwin, the eminent English scientist, came in contact with the Terre del Fuegans in their gross degradation, he publicly declared that here was a people to whom it was vain to send missionaries, as the gospel could not do anything for them. But brave men of God went there and took the gospel to them in the power of the Holy Spirit, and demonstrated that it met the need of the Terre del Fuegans, with such great results that Charles Darwin publicly admitted his mistake and became a regular subscriber to the work.

The gospel, *with a crucified Christ as its center,* meets the needs of all conditions and classes of men as well as of all races. It meets the need of the millionaire and the need of the pauper; it meets the need of great men of science like James D. Dana and Lord Kelvin, and the need of the man or woman who cannot read nor write; it meets the need of the king on the throne and the need of the laborer in the ditch. I myself have seen with my own eyes noblemen and servant girls, university deans and men who could scarcely read, prisoners in penitentiaries and leaders in moral uplift, brilliant lawyers and dull plodding workingmen, come under its attraction, and saved by its power. But it was only because I made *"Christ crucified,"* His atoning work, the center of my preaching.

4. Fourth, the words *"unto me." "I will draw all men* ***unto me.****"* The Revised Version reads *"Unto* ***myself,****"* and that was just what Jesus said, *"And I, if I be lifted up from the earth, will draw all men* ***unto myself.****"* It is not to a creed or a system of doctrine that Jesus draws men, but to a Person, to Himself. That is what we need, a Person, Jesus Himself. As He Himself once said, *"Come* ***unto***

***me**, all ye that labour and are heavy laden, and I will give you rest"* (Matthew 11:28). Creeds and confessions of faith are all right in their place. They are of great value. The organized church is of great value. It is indispensable, and it is the most important institution in the world today. Society would soon go to rack and ruin without it. We are all under solemn obligation to God and to our fellowman to support it and belong to it, but creeds and confessions of faith cannot save. The church cannot save. A divine Person can save, Jesus Christ, and He alone. So He says, *"And I, if I be lifted up from the earth, will draw all men **unto myself**."*

II. Why Christ Lifted Up on the Cross Draws All Men unto Himself

But why does Christ lifted up on the cross, the crucified Christ, draw all men unto Himself? There are two reasons why Christ lifted up, and Christ *crucified* draws all men unto Himself.

1. Christ crucified draws all men unto Himself because Christ crucified meets the first, the deepest, the greatest, and most fundamental need of man. What is man's first, greatest, deepest, most fundamental need? A Savior? A Savior from what? First of all, and underlying all else, a Savior from the guilt of sin. Every man of every race has sinned. As Paul put it in Romans 3:22–23, *"There is no difference: for all have sinned, and come short of the glory of God."* There is no difference between Jew and Gentile, at this point, nor is there any difference between English and German at this point. There is no difference between American and Japanese at this point, no difference between European and Asian, no difference between the American and the African. "There is no difference: for **all** have sinned, and come short of the glory of God." Every man of every race is a sinner. "There is no difference" at this point. And every man shall have to answer for his sin to the infinitely holy God who rules this universe.

Therefore, all men need an atoning Savior, who can by His atoning death make propitiation for, and so cover up, our sins, and thus reconcile us to this holy God, deliver us from His awful wrath, and bring us out into the glorious sunlight of His favor. And Jesus lifted up is the only atoning Savior in the universe. He who alone was at the same time God and man, He alone can make atonement for sin; and He has made it, has made a perfect atonement, and God has accepted His atonement and testified to His acceptance of His atonement by raising Him from the dead. The Lord Jesus actually meets our need. He actually meets every man's first, greatest, deepest, most fundamental need, and He alone.

In the entire universe, there is no other religion except Christianity that even offers an atoning Savior. Mohammedanism offers Mohammed, "The Prophet," a teacher, but not a Savior; Buddhism offers Buddha, supposedly at least a wonderful teacher, "The Light of Asia," but not an atoning Savior; Confucianism offers Confucius, a marvelous teacher far ahead of his time, but not an atoning Savior. No religion offers an atoning Savior, offers an atonement of any real character, except Christianity. This is the radical point of difference between Christianity and every other religion in the world, yet some fool preachers are trying to eliminate from Christianity this, its very point of radical difference from all other religions. But such an emasculated Christianity will not reach the needs of men and will not draw men. It never has and it never will. The Bible and history are at one at this point. Jesus Christ offers Himself lifted up on the cross to redeem us from the curse of the law, by "becoming a curse in our behalf." "*Christ hath redeemed us from the curse of the law, being made a curse for us: for it is written, Cursed is every one that hangeth on a tree*" (Galatians 3:13). Men know their need; they may try to forget it. They may try to deny it. They may try to drown their sense of it by drink and dissipation or by wild pleasure-seeking or wild money-getting, or by listening to fake preachers in supposedly orthodox pulpits, like one who in this city declared recently that, "the old sense of sin is fast disappearing," and added, "the change is for the better not for the worse." He spoke also of "imaginary and artificial sins like 'the sin of unbelief,'" and then went on to say, "In this we agree with Christ," apparently not knowing enough about the Bible to know that Jesus Himself was the very one who said in John 16:8–9, *"And he, when he is come, will convict the world in respect of sin, and of righteousness, and of judgment; of sin,* ***because they believe not on me****"* (ASV).

But in spite of all our attempts to drown or stupefy or silence our sense of sin, our consciousness of guilt before a Holy God, we all have it, and like Banquo's Ghost, it will not down. Nothing gives the guilty conscience abiding peace but the atoning blood of Jesus Christ. And so, Christ *lifted up* draws all men unto Him, and even wicked ministers of Satan, like the preacher I have just referred to, sometimes come to their senses and flee to the real Christ, *Christ crucified,* as I hope this one may. Yes, Jesus, Jesus only, Jesus *lifted up on the cross,* Jesus crucified for our sins, making full atonement for our sins. He and He alone meets the deepest need of us all, and so His cross draws us all unto Himself. Happy is the man or the woman who yields to that drawing. Woe to the man or woman who resists that drawing; final gloom, despondency, and despair are their lot. Oh, how many men and women who have gotten their eyes opened to see the facts, to see their awful guilt, and who have been plunged into deepest consequent despair, have come to me, and I have pointed them to *Jesus on the cross,* and have shown them by God's Word all their sins laid upon Him and thus settled, and they have come to Him, and believed God's testimony about Him, that He had borne all their sins in His own body on the cross, and they have found perfect peace and boundless joy. And that is the only way to find perfect peace and boundless joy.

Will you set out to find peace? If you do not, great gloom, utter despair, awaits you someday, in this world or in the world to come.

In my first pastorate, I tried to get a man to come to Christ lifted up to meet his need of pardon; but though it was many years ago, he held to the theology that is preached as "new theology" today, and sought to still the voice of conscience, and stupefy his sense of sin by denying his guilt and his need of an atoning Savior. He did not wish to listen to me or to see me. But the hour came when death drew nigh. A cancer was eating its way through scalp and skull into his brain. Then he cried to those about his dying bed, "Send for Mr. Torrey." I hurried to his side. He was in despair. "Oh!" he said. "Dr. Tidhall tells me that I have but a short time to live, that as soon as this cancer gets a little further and eats through the thin film of skull and touches the brain, I am a dead man. Tell me how to be saved." I sat down beside him, and told him what to do to be saved. I tried to make as plain as I knew how the way of salvation through the *uplifted Christ,* Christ uplifted on the cross. I think I know how to make it plain, but he had waited too long. He could not grasp it. I stayed with him. Night came on. I said to his family, "You have been up night after night with him. I will sit with him tonight." They instructed me what to do, how to minister to him. Time after time during the night I had to go to another room to get some nourishment for him, and as I would come back into the room where he lay, from his bed in the corner there would rise the constant cry, "Oh, I wish I were a Christian. Oh, I wish I were a Christian. Oh, I wish I were a Christian." And thus he died.

2. Christ lifted up on the cross, Christ crucified, draws all men unto Him, because lifted up there to die for us He reveals His wonderful love, and the wondrous love of the Father far us. *"Hereby perceive we the love of God, because he laid down his life for us"* (1 John 3:16), and *"God commendeth his love toward us, in that, while we were yet sinners,* ***Christ died for us****"* (Romans 5:8). There is nothing that draws men like Love. Love draws all men in every clime. But no other love draws like the love of God. John 3:16, *"For God so loved the world, that he gave his only begotten Son, that*

whosoever believeth in him should not perish, but have everlasting life," has broken thousands of hard hearts.

One night, preaching in my own church in Minneapolis, the whole choir stayed for the after-meeting. The leading soprano was an intelligent young woman but living a worldly life. She remained with the rest. In the after-meeting, her mother arose in the back of the church and said, "I wish you would pray for the conversion of my daughter." I did not look around but knew instinctively that her cheeks were flushing, and her eyes flashing with anger. As soon as the meeting was dismissed, I hurried down so that I could meet her before she got out of the church. As she came toward me, I held out my hand to her. She stamped her foot, and with flashing eyes cried, "Mr. Torrey, my mother knows better than to do that. She knows it will only make me worse." I said, "Sit down, Cora." She sat down, and without any argument I opened my Bible to Isaiah 53:5, and began to read, *"But he was wounded for our transgressions, he was bruised for our iniquities: the chastisement of our peace was upon him; and with his stripes we are healed."* She burst into tears, and the next night accepted Jesus Christ. I had to go to Duluth for a few days, and when I returned, I found that she was seriously ill. One morning, her brother came hurrying up to my home and said that she was apparently dying, that she was unconscious, and white from the loss of blood. I hastened down, and as I entered the room, she lay there with her eyes closed, with the whitest face I ever saw on one who was not actually dead. She was apparently unconscious, scarcely breathing. I knelt by her side to pray, more for the sake of the mother who stood beside the bed than for her, for I supposed that she was beyond help or hearing. But no sooner had I finished my prayer, than in a clear, full, richly musical tone she began to pray. These were about her words, "Heavenly Father, if it be Your will, raise me up that as I have used my voice for myself and only to please myself, I may use my voice for Your glory, but if in Your wisdom You see that it is best for me not to live, I shall be glad to go to be with Christ," and she went to be with Christ.

Oh, I have seen thousands melted as I have repeated to them and shown them the picture of Christ on the cross, as told in Isaiah 53:5, *"But he was wounded for our transgressions, he was bruised for our iniquities: the chastisement of our peace was upon him; and with his stripes we are healed."*

A few days ago, I received a missionary magazine containing a testimony from one who was going to Egypt under the Egypt General Mission. This young missionary said, "When I was twelve years old, during the Torrey-Alexander meetings, in 1904, I gave my heart to the Lord Jesus Christ. Dr. Torrey was speaking on Isaiah 53:5, and he asked us to repeat the words with him, but changing the word 'our' into the word 'my.' While repeating the text in this way, I suddenly realized, as if for the first time, that Jesus had really suffered all this for me, and there and then I gave my life to Him."

Oh I men and women, look now! See Jesus Christ lifted up on the cross, see Him hanging on that awful cross, see Him wounded for your transgressions, bruised for your iniquities, and the chastisement of your peace laid on Him. Oh, men and women living in sin, men and women rejecting Christ for the world, men and women who have looked to the lies of Christian Science, Unitarianism and other systems that deny His atoning blood, listen! *"But he was wounded for our transgressions, he was bruised for our iniquities: the chastisement of our peace was upon him; and with his stripes we are healed."* Won't you yield to that love, won't you give up your sin, give up your worldly pleasures, give up your willful errors, and accept the Savior who loves you, and died for you, who was *"wounded for your transgressions,...bruised for your iniquities"* and upon whom the chastisement of your peace was laid? Accept Him right now.

6

THE MOST IMPORTANT QUESTION OF THE DAY

"What shall I do then with Jesus which is called Christ?"
—Matthew 27:22

If I were to put this question to the audience tonight, What is the most important question of the day, I presume I would get a great variety of answers. Some of you would say that the Disarmament question or the Four Power Treaty question was the most important question of the day. Some would say that the Labor question was the most important question of the day. And still others would say that the Prohibition question was the most important question of the day, and so on. But all these answers would be wrong. There is another question of vastly more importance than any one of these, a question of which immeasurably more depends upon the right decision than upon the decision of any of these questions. That question is this, *"What shall I do with Jesus, who is called Christ?"* (Matthew 27:22).

It is not a new question. Pontius Pilate asked it nearly nineteen hundred years ago, and answered it wrong, and his earthly life went out in darkness, and his eternity was blasted. Thousands upon thousands have asked it since. Everything that is really worth having for time and for eternity depends upon a right decision of that question for each one of us. If you do the right thing with Jesus, the Christ of God, you will get everything that is really worth having for time as well as for eternity, whether a right decision is given on these various other questions or not. If you do the wrong thing with Jesus, the Christ of God, you will lose everything that is worth having for time as well as for eternity, even though all these other questions are decided as they should be.

I. What We Will Get if We Do the Right Thing with Jesus Christ?

Let us look at some of the things that we will get if we do the right thing with Jesus Christ.

1. First, if you do the right thing with Jesus, you will get the forgiveness of all your sins. Saint Peter said in Acts 10:43, "*To him all the prophets witness, that through his name* ***every one*** *that* ***believeth on him shall receive remission of sins***" (ASV). Now this statement is as plain as day, and in it God's inspired apostle declares that "*every one that believeth on*" Jesus Christ, "*shall receive remission of* [his] *sins.*" If the vilest sinner on earth would come in here tonight and would put his trust in Jesus Christ, the moment he did it, all his sins would be forgiven, blotted out.

The forgiveness of our sins depends solely upon what we do with Jesus Christ. It does not depend upon our prayers or upon our penances or upon our good works. If you do the right thing with Jesus Christ, you get forgiveness of all your sins whatever else you may do or not do. If you do the wrong thing with Jesus Christ, you will not get forgiveness of sins whatever else you may do or not do. The same truth is put in a different way in John 3:18, *"He that believeth on him is not condemned: but he that believeth not is condemned already, because he hath not believed in the name of the only begotten Son of God."*

What an unspeakable blessing the forgiveness of all your sins is. Wealth, honors, or pleasures are not so eagerly to be desired as the forgiveness of our sins. All of them together are not to be compared with the forgiveness of our sins. Forgiveness of sin brings joy anywhere it comes, whether it is into the palace or into the prison cell. King David had wealth, honor, power, pleasures, and privileges without number, but he was not happy. Indeed he was perfectly miserable. His own description of his condition is found in the Thirty-second Psalm, the third and fourth verses: *"When I kept silence, my bones waxed old through my roaring all the day long. For day and night thy hand was heavy upon me: my moisture is turned into the drought of summer."* Then he found forgiveness of sin and in his joy he shouted, *"Blessed is he whose transgression is forgiven, whose sin is covered. Blessed is the man unto whom the Lord imputeth not iniquity"* (Psalm 32:1–2).

Down in a wretched cell in Sing Sing prison, there was a man under a fifteen-year sentence for manslaughter. He was, of course, a very unhappy man. But there in his cell he got hold of a Bible and read it, and the Holy Spirit through the Bible showed him the Lord Jesus as his Savior who died in his place, and he accepted Jesus Christ as his Savior. It was in the middle of the night when he finally found the Savior through meditating on what he had read in the Word of God, and though it was in the middle of the night and in a prison cell, such joy came into his soul that he began to shout. The guard came along and rapped on his door and told him to keep still. "I can't keep still," he shouted back. "My sins are forgiven." Yes, there is a more wonderful joy in knowing that our sins are all forgiven than there is in anything that this world has to give. And *we get this forgiveness of sin by simply believing on the Lord Jesus Christ.*

2. Second, *you will get peace of conscience by doing the right thing with Jesus Christ.* It is a blessed thing to have a conscience that does not accuse you, a conscience that has found perfect peace. It is an awful thing to have a conscience that does accuse. It is the greatest misery on earth. It drives many men and many women to suicide. Oh, in what agony of mind men and women have come to me from different ranks of society because of an accusing conscience. And there are many who never unburden their hearts to others who are in misery from the same cause. There are men and women here tonight who spend days and nights of misery because of an accusing conscience. You try to drown the voice of conscience in many ways, but you fail utterly. You try to drown the voice of conscience in pleasure and dissipation. You try to drown the voice of conscience in business. You try to drown the voice of conscience in drink and in dope, and in other ways; but you do not succeed. You never will succeed.

One who perhaps knows as much about the life of the Movie Colony in Hollywood as anyone else told a friend of mine a few weeks ago of two of the leading stars in the movie world, two women whose names are constantly in the daily papers and who are admired and envied by thousands, that they were the hopeless slaves of dope. All over this land people who are counted gifted, and on whom others look in envy, are trying to silence the voice of conscience by dope. But no one ever yet found real peace in that way, and no one ever will. Jesus Christ alone can give the guilty conscience peace. In Romans 5:1, God put it through the apostle Paul in this way, "*Being justified by faith,* ***we have peace with God through our Lord Jesus Christ.***" Do the right thing with Jesus Christ, and you will get true peace of conscience, deep, abiding peace, perfect peace. As Isaiah put it, *"Thou wilt keep him in perfect peace, whose mind is stayed on thee:* ***because he trusteth in thee****"* (Isaiah 26:3). But do the wrong thing with Jesus Christ, and you cannot find peace of conscience in this world or in the next, no matter what else you may do to get peace.

I was dealing once in my office with a woman who told me that she had been in a perfect hell through an accusing conscience for fourteen years. I pointed her to Jesus Christ. I showed her from God's Word how all her sins had been laid upon Jesus Christ. She believed it. She took God's Word for it, and put her trust in Him as her atoning Savior. After fourteen years of agony, of hell on earth, she went out from my office that day with a radiant countenance; for she had found peace of conscience in the only way in which peace of conscience can ever be found by anybody, through her Lord Jesus Christ. And that joy continues until this day.

3. Third, *you will get deliverance from the power of sin by doing the right thing with Jesus Christ.* It is a dreadful thing to be in the power of sin. There is no other slavery so binding, so degrading, and so crushing as the slavery of sin. We all know what a dreadful thing it is to be in the power of some sins. We all know, for example, what an awful thing it is to be in the power of strong drink. We know what an awful thing it is to be in the power of morphine, or cocaine, or some other kind of dope. Many of us know through stories, distressing and agonizing, that have been poured into our ears, what an awful thing it is to be in the power of lust. How many men have come to me in despair this past year and told the story of their dreadful slavery. It is an awful thing to be in the power of sin of any kind.

There is, however, a way to get free. There is a way by which any man or woman who is the slave of any sin of any kind can get instantaneous and complete deliverance from the power of that sin. There is, however, only one way. That way is by doing the right thing with Jesus Christ. The apostle Paul was once in the power of sin. He was once helpless and hopelessly enslaved. With all the power of an unusually strong will, he tried to break away from the power of sin, but the more he tried to break away, the more completely he seemed to be in sin's grip forever, until at last in utter despair he cried, *"O wretched man that I am! who shall deliver me from the body of this death?"* (Romans 7:24). And then he found Christ and took Him as his Deliverer from the power of sin, and he found perfect freedom and cried again, *"I thank God through Jesus Christ our Lord"* (verse 25). You cannot get out of sin's power unless you do the right thing with Jesus Christ. You may get free from some bad habits. You may, for example, give up drinking without the help of Christ, though very few do; but whether you do or do not, you will not get out of sin's grip. It will simply turn from one sin to another. Christ alone can save you from sin's power. I could stand here by the hour and tell you of men and women I have personally known, men and women as completely enslaved by sin in one form or another as any man or woman who ever walked the earth, whom the Lord Jesus Christ has set free when they did the right thing with Him.

4. Fourth, You will get great joy by doing the right thing with Jesus Christ. The apostle Peter said in 1 Peter 1:8, *"In whom, though now ye see him not, yet believing, ye rejoice with joy unspeakable and full of glory."* You can get "joy unspeakable and full of glory" by doing the right thing with Jesus Christ. You cannot get joy unspeakable and full of glory in any other way. You know happy people, of course, who are not Christians, but you do not know anyone who is not a Christian who has "joy unspeakable and full of glory." You do not know anyone who is not a Christian who has the deep, constant, satisfying, and overflowing joy, that those men and women have who are not merely nominal Christians but real Christians—those men and women who have fully accepted Christ as their personal Savior and are really trusting God for the

forgiveness of all their sins because they fully, believe God's testimony concerning Jesus Christ having borne every one of their sins when He died on the cross, thus fully settling their sins forever, and who have without reservation surrendered the entire control of their thoughts and lives to Jesus Christ, and who are confessing Jesus Christ as their Lord before the world every reasonable opportunity they get, and who are watching for every opportunity to lead others to Christ, and who are serving Jesus Christ with all their strength every day.

Do the right thing with Jesus Christ and you get this wonderful joy. Reject Jesus Christ and you lose it. How foolish men and women are! There are many men in this audience tonight who are rejecting Christ because they think they will lose joy if they take Christ. Are you blind, men? Do you not see that those who have taken Christ really are happier than you are? Do you not see that many Christians are happier in poverty than skeptics and worldlings are in wealth? Are you deaf, women? Have you not heard many whose word you must believe, and from all ranks of society, testify that they have found a joy since they took Christ that they never dreamed of in the world?

I do not think that many of you could tell me much that I do not know about this world's joys. I have tasted them pretty much all, but I never knew *"joy unspeakable and full of glory"* until I took Jesus Christ. I do now. My every day is full of joy. I have perplexities. I have annoyances. I have experiences that could easily prove exasperating. I have burdens of many kinds. I have what may appear to be great losses. I have things said to me and written to me, and said and printed about me, that would cut to the quick if I did not know the Lord Jesus. But through it all, every day is unspeakably happy. Not so long ago, I had more things come to me that might have caused grief and anxiety and worry and heartache and deep sorrow than in almost any other week of my life, but it was a radiantly happy week. Why? Simply because of what Jesus Christ is to me, and what He is to me just because I have done the right thing with Him.

5. Fifth, *If you do the right thing with Jesus Christ, you will get eternal life.* Eternal Life! What a wonderful phrase that is, Eternal Life. Life that never ends! Life that knows no death! Life of unutterable beauty and dignity and honor and glory and rapture! Life that is endless in its duration and perfect in its quality! Life like the life of God Himself. *Eternal life!* What does the world have to put in comparison with that? What is the wealth of a John D. Rockefeller or a Henry Ford compared with eternal life? I would rather be a penniless pauper all my days, living in destitution and hunger and rags and cold, and have eternal life, than to roll in wealth all my days and have all that wealth can buy, and not have eternal life. I have no envy for the rich. No; I know their lives and hearts too well. I have often a greater pity for them than for the poor; for they are often more to be pitied than the poor. The life of the average millionaire is a sad, sad life.

What is the wisdom of an Edison, or of the world's greatest scientist or philosopher, compared with eternal life? What are the honors of a great general or a mighty ruler of men compared with eternal life? What are the pleasures of the most successful votary of pleasure compared with eternal life? Put all the world has, absolutely everything the world can give, into one pan of the scales. Put eternal life into the other scale. See the world's side go up. It is lighter than the smallest dust of the balance in comparison with Eternal Life. Eternal Life! Oh, who can fathom all the depth of meaning that there is in these two wondrous words?

And you get it by simply doing the right thing with Jesus Christ. Do the right thing with Jesus Christ and you get eternal life. Do the wrong thing with Jesus Christ and you lose eternal life. Listen to God's own Word about that, John 3:36, *"He that believeth on the Son* ***hath eternal life:*** *and he that believeth not the Son* ***shall not see life;*** *but the wrath of God abideth on him."* Listen to God's Word again, *"And the witness is this, that God gave unto us eternal life,* ***and this life is in his Son.*** *He* ***that hath the Son hath the life;*** *he that hath not the Son of God hath not the life"* (1 John 5:11–12 ASV).

Are you going to do the right thing with Jesus Christ tonight and get eternal life, or are you going to do the wrong thing with Jesus Christ and forever lose eternal life?

6. Sixth, there is something better even than eternal life that you get by doing the right thing with Jesus Christ. *By doing the right thing with Jesus Christ, you become a child of God, an heir of God and joint heir with Jesus Christ.* We read in God's own Word in John 1:12, *"As many as* ***received him,*** *to them gave he the* ***right to become children of God,*** *even to them that believe on his name."* And in Romans 8:17, we read, *"If children, then heirs; heirs of God, and joint-heirs with Christ."* Just think of that a moment, a child of God, and an heir of God, and a joint heir (or fellow-heir) with Jesus Christ. We have heard these words very often, but have we ever stopped to weigh their meaning and to take in their wondrous import? *A child of God!* Think of it! God the infinite One; God the Creator of all things; God to whom the whole race of men and the whole company of angels is as nothing, less than a speck of dust is in comparison to the whole earth; God in comparison with whom the greatest of philosophers, the mightiest of monarchs, and the purest of saints is less than the most ignorant idiot is in comparison with the greatest philosopher: and we to become His children and His heirs! Heirs of all this infinite God is and all this infinite God has. It almost staggers the mind to try to think of it. That is what is open to each one of us. That is what is open to you and open to me by just doing the right thing with Jesus Christ.

One day, years ago, I met the son and heir of one of the richest men in the whole world, and he invited me to dinner. As I sat and talked with him, it seemed to me as if it might be in some respects a fine thing to be the son and heir of the richest millionaire on earth. But that is nothing, just nothing at all to being a child of God, an heir of God and fellow-heir with Jesus Christ. That is what is open to us, to each one of us; but it can be obtained in only one way, and that is by doing the right thing with Jesus Christ. Do the right thing with Jesus Christ and in a moment you become a child of God, an heir of God and fellow-heir with Jesus Christ. Listen to God's own statement about it again. *"As many as received him, to them gave he the right to become children of God, even to them that believe on his name"* (John 1:12).

Do the wrong thing with Jesus Christ and you lose forever your chance of becoming a child of God, an heir of God and a fellow-heir with Jesus Christ. Oh, what a loss that is! The loss of untold wealth, the loss of earth's greatest honors, the loss of dearest friends, is nothing in comparison with the loss of becoming a child of God, an heir of God, and a fellow-heir with Jesus Christ. That is the awful cost of doing the wrong thing with Jesus Christ. We see then something of what we gain by doing the right thing with Jesus Christ, and something of what we lose by doing the wrong thing with Jesus Christ. By doing the right thing with Jesus Christ we gain Forgiveness of all our sins. By doing the right thing with Jesus Christ we gain Peace of Conscience. By doing the right thing with Jesus Christ we gain deliverance from sin's power. By doing the right thing with Jesus Christ we gain joy unspeakable and full of glory. By doing the right thing with Jesus Christ we gain eternal life. By doing the right thing with Jesus Christ we become children of God, heirs of God, and fellow-heirs with Jesus Christ. Is it not evident then that the most important question of this day and of all days is, *"What shall I do then with Jesus which is called Christ?"*

But what will *you* do with Him? Will you do the right thing with Him, or will you do the wrong thing with Him? Will you do the right thing and gain all, or will you do the wrong thing and lose all? I put the question to each individual reader. What will you do with Jesus? It does not matter whether you are a church member or not. I put the question to you. What will you do with Jesus? I put the question to the most worldly man or woman here, as well as to the most religious, "What will you do with Jesus who is called Christ?" I put the question to the one who is most sunken in sin; for there is hope for you of getting all these things if you do the right thing with Jesus Christ, just as much as there is for the most moral and upright and highly respected man or woman here. "What then will you do with Jesus, which is called Christ?" Of each one of you I ask, Will you do the right thing with Jesus Christ, or will you do the wrong thing with Jesus Christ?

7. Seventh, there is something better than anything I have mentioned yet that depends entirely upon what you do with Jesus Christ. *If you do the right thing with Jesus Christ, then someday you will become just like Him.* Listen to what God says, *"Behold, what manner of love the Father hath bestowed upon us, that we should be called the children of God: and such we are....Beloved, now are we the children of God, and it is not yet made manifest what we shall be. We know that, when he shall be manifested, **we shall be like him;** for we shall see him even as he is"* (1 John 3:1–2 ASV). "What?" someone will say, "can I become like Jesus Christ?" Yes, even *you* can become just like Jesus Christ. Think of it! You and I with all our present failings, with all our shortcomings, meanness, and pettiness, some of which we do not see but others see very clearly, for they stick out all over us and generally, they stick out most conspicuously upon those of us who have the best opinion of ourselves. But even *we* can become just like Him, be like Him in every perfection and glory of His matchless, faultless, glorious, divine character. Yes, and we can be like Him in the glory of His outward appearance too; for it is written in the Word of God, *"For our citizenship is in heaven; from whence also we wait for a Savior, the Lord Jesus Christ: who **shall fashion anew the***

***body** of our humiliation, **that it may be conformed to the body of his glory**, according to the working whereby he is able even to subject all things unto himself*" (Philippians 3:20–21 ASV). And how can we become just like Him? By doing the right thing with Jesus Christ.

II. What Is the Right Thing to Do with Jesus Christ?

But what is the right thing to do with Jesus Christ?

1. The right thing to do with Jesus Christ is to receive Him, to receive Him as your Savior. This is evident from the verse that we have quoted already a number of times, John 1:12, "*As many as **received him**, to them gave he the right to become children of God, even to them that believe on his name*" (ASV). He died for your sins. "*All we like sheep have gone astray; we have turned every one to his own way; and the LORD hath made to strike on him the iniquity of us all*" (Isaiah 53:6). Will you accept Him as your sin-bearer? Will you say, "Oh God, I believe what Your Word says about Jesus Christ. I believe He bore my sins in His own body on the cross. I believe every one of my sins was laid upon Him and settled fully and forever when He died on the cross in my place. And I now take Him as my sin-bearer. Forgive all my sins for Jesus Christ's sake"?

Take Him not only as your Savior from the guilt of sin but also take Him as your Savior from the power of sin. He not only died to make atonement for your sins, He also rose again, and He lives today to set you free from the power of sin and to make intercession for you. (See Hebrews 7:25.) Will you take Him tonight as your Deliverer from the power of sin? Will you come to this risen and mighty Lord Jesus with all your weakness and sins and trust Him to set you free? That is the right thing to do with Jesus Christ: just take Him as your Savior, your crucified Savior from the guilt of sin and your risen Savior from the power of sin.

2. The next right thing to do with Jesus is to let Him into your heart. He says, "*Behold, I stand at the door, and knock: if any man hear my voice, and open the door, I will come in to him, and will sup with him, and he with me*" (Revelation 3:20). Jesus is standing at the door of every heart. He is knocking at the door of every heart. Will you open the door and let Him in? Who will? Who will say, "Lord Jesus, come in. Come in and reign."

3. The next right thing to do with Jesus is to *enthrone Him in your heart*. He is the Christ, God's anointed King, because God has made Him so. As Peter said on the Day of Pentecost, "*God hath made him both Lord and Christ, this Jesus whom ye crucified*" (Acts 2:36 ASV). Will you enthrone Him as King in your heart? Will you say honestly to Him, "Lord Jesus, take the throne of my heart and live and reign there supreme." Who will do it?

4. Once more, the right thing to do with Jesus Christ is to confess Him before the world as your Lord and Master. He Himself says in Matthew 10:32–33, "*Every one therefore who shall confess me before men, him will I also confess before my Father which is in heaven. But whosoever shall deny me before men, him will I also deny before my Father which is in heaven*" (ASV). And Paul says in Romans 10:9–10, "*If thou shalt confess with thy mouth Jesus as Lord, and shalt believe in thy heart that God raised him from the dead, thou shalt be saved: for with the heart man believeth unto righteousness; and with the mouth confession is made unto salvation*" (ASV). Who will do it?

There is just one more right thing to do with Jesus. What is it? Go tell others about Him, when you yourself have taken Him as your Savior, and let Him into your heart, and enthroned Him as King, and confessed Him before the world as your Lord.

When Jesus was here on earth, He cast several thousand demons out of a wretched man who was in their control. The condition of that man before he met Jesus was awful beyond description, but the condition of that man after he met Jesus was glorious beyond description. And that man naturally wanted to go with Jesus wherever He went. But Jesus said, in effect, "No, do not go away with me, but stay right here and go to your home, and declare how great things God hath done for thee." "*And he went his way publishing throughout the whole city how great things Jesus had done for him*" (Luke 8:38–39).

Oh, if you have taken Jesus, go tell everyone you can about Him and bring every one you can to Him.

These are the right things to do with Jesus. Who will do them tonight and gain all that is worth having for time and for eternity? Who will take Him as your Savior? Who will listen to His voice and let Him into your heart? Who will enthrone Him in his heart as King? Who will begin the confession of Him as your Lord?

7

GREAT THINGS AND HOW ANYONE CAN GET THEM

"All things are yours."
—1 Corinthians 3:21

You will find my text in 1 Corinthians 3:21, *"All things are yours."* That is a text that stirs the blood. I pity any man who is not stirred to the very depths of his being by an utterance of God like that, *"All things are yours."* There are many who think that only a few men can ever attain great things, that the great mass of men must rest content with small things, with things of little account. That is not so. The very greatest things, indeed everything that is of infinite and eternal value is open to all men. There is not a man or woman here tonight who cannot have great things, the very greatest things, those things that are of most priceless worth. Certainly, if anyone will become a member of that class of people to whom God, in our text, makes the marvelous promise, *"All things are yours,"* he can have the very greatest things, those things that are of most priceless value.

I. Great Joy

Anyone here can have great joy. When Christ was born at Bethlehem, an angel came down from heaven and proclaimed, *"Behold, I bring you good tidings of great joy, which shall be to all people. For unto you is born this day in the city of David a Savior, who is Christ the Lord"* (Luke 2:10–11). The birth of Jesus, the Christ of God, into this world brought great joy into the world: the reception of Jesus Christ as Savior and Lord by the individual man or woman brings great joy into the heart of that man or woman. No matter who the man or woman may be who receives Jesus Christ, he will find joy, great joy in Him. The highest form of joy known to man is joy in the Lord Jesus. The Lord Jesus fills every heart into which He is admitted with boundless joy. One may be very gloomy and despondent by nature, but if he really receives Jesus Christ, he will find great joy.

I recall a man who I think was one of the gloomiest men I ever met. He had one of those despondent, despairing faces that make you shudder. I dreaded to have him approach me. The man had at one time been the inmate of an insane asylum where he was sent for melancholia, and he looked and acted as if he ought to be there still. It was my privilege to point that man to Jesus Christ. He did not accept Jesus Christ in a day. I dealt with him day after day for quite a while, and he seemed so deeply immersed in his gloom that the light could not penetrate his darkened heart. It seemed as if he never would see the truth and accept the Lord Jesus. He was one of the most discouraging men with whom I have ever dealt. But he kept coming back to me, and at last, by the power of the Holy Spirit, the light broke in upon his darkened heart and he received Jesus Christ, and became at once one of the brightest, happiest men I ever knew, as well as one of the most faithful and effective Christian workers.

I met another man who had made a shipwreck of life. He belonged to a good family. He was a man of unusual ability and well educated. But he had gone wrong and had thrown away his life in sin. The night I first met him, he was a wanderer on the face of the earth, hundreds of miles from home, money gone, friends gone, manhood gone, and seemingly everything worthwhile gone. He came to me at the close of a service I was conducting and asked me if I thought there was any hope for a man like him? I told him, "Yes," that I knew that there was, and pointed him to the Lord Jesus, and he took Him that night and became a very happy man. That was years ago, but for many years, every now and then, I got a letter from him telling me of his great joy. He is happy indeed, today; for he is with Christ in glory.

No one who ever really took Jesus Christ, rich or poor, learned or ignorant, moral or vicious, honest or criminal, of any nation or character, did not find great joy. God has provided great joy for everyone in Jesus Christ. I know a man at the present time in San Quentin for murder, but after he had already been in San Quentin for some years, he was led to accept the Lord Jesus Christ. His letters, some of which his father lets me see, are among the most joyous letters, and the most full of Jesus Christ, of any letters I have even seen.

If anyone does not have great joy, it is wholly his own fault. No one can rob another of his joy if his joy is really in Jesus Christ. Men may rob you of your money, they may rob you of your good name, and they may rob you of your friends, but they cannot rob you of your joy, if it really is in the Lord Jesus.

I met a woman in Chicago many years ago. She was most wretched. She had had great misfortunes come into her life. She had been defrauded of her money. She had been robbed of her husband and his love. Her soul was bitter. She had a hard, sour face—one of the hardest faces I ever saw. I spoke to her about Jesus

Christ. She would not listen. She hated the one who had wronged her and longed to get even, and would not listen to the story of the love of God. She said God did not love her or He would never have permitted her to suffer what she had suffered. I met the same woman again in the Moody Church some years later. Again, I spoke to her of Jesus Christ and of God's love. This time she professed to be an infidel. I knew she was lying to me and told her so, and recalled her story as she had told it to me several years before. She supposed that I had forgotten her and so had ventured on this new story that she was an infidel. But she was still hard and bitter. A year or two later I met her again. Again I spoke to her of Jesus Christ, and this time she broke down and accepted Him. Immediately, her life was changed. Instead of bitterness, she found great joy at once. I met her again sometime later. She had been very sick but was still rejoicing in Jesus Christ and longing to tell others of this wonderful Savior and the joy He brings into the heart of those who accept Him.

I was once sitting in my office in Minneapolis and a woman with a very hard face came in. She approached my desk and said, "Do you send missionaries to talk with people who are dying?" "Yes," I replied. "Well, there is a woman dying at my house" (and she gave me the street and number). "I wish you would send a missionary around to talk to her." I judged from the woman's appearance the kind of place it must be and the kind of woman it must be who was dying. In a little while, two women missionaries came in. I said to them, "There is a woman dying at such and such a street and number. Will you go around and talk with her? I think it is a wicked place and that the woman has lived a life of sin."

The two missionaries went aside and prayed and then went around to this house. It was as I had suspected, a den of infamy, and the dying woman was a woman who had made the worst shipwreck of life that a woman can make. They told the dying woman of Jesus Christ and His death for her upon the cross of Calvary, and how He had made full atonement for all her sins. And then she received Jesus Christ and great joy at once came into the heart that sin had so darkened.

When the missionaries came back I asked them, "Did she accept Jesus Christ?"

"Yes," they said, "but that is not all, Mr. Torrey. Though she was dying of an incurable disease that no physician could heal, we were led to kneel down and pray that God would not only save her soul but would also heal her body. God heard our prayer, and she is healed."

The woman was beyond any human physician's skill, but these missionaries had been given faith to pray for her recovery from an incurable and loathsome disease. God had heard their prayer. She got up from that bed, a saved, happy, and well woman. Years afterward, when I had moved to Chicago, one of these two missionaries came to Chicago to study at the Moody Institute, and this woman heard that she was coming and came to her and told her to bring me a message of her joy in the Lord.

Oh, there is great joy for everybody, if they will only seek it in God's way. Anyone can have it. If you wish it, come to me at the close of this service and I will tell you just what to do to get it.

We are told in Acts 8:8, that when Samaria received the truth regarding the Lord Jesus Christ, *"there was great joy in that city."* If anyone will receive the truth regarding Jesus Christ and receive Jesus Christ Himself into his heart, there will be *"great joy"* in that heart.

II. Great Peace

But there is another great thing anyone here can have. You can have *great peace*. Peace and joy are closely related, but they are not the same thing by any means. But they are to be obtained in much the same way. If we accept Jesus Christ, and trust in Him, and obey His Word, we shall have great peace as well as great joy. Paul said in Philippians 4:6–7, *"In nothing be anxious; but in everything by prayer and supplication with thanksgiving let your requests be made known to God.* ***And the peace of God, which passeth all understanding, shall guard your hearts and your thoughts in Christ Jesus"*** (ASV). And the experience of thousands and tens of thousands of people proves this promise that God made through Paul, to be absolutely true.

Think of that! ***"The peace of God,*** *which passeth* ***all understanding."*** Is not that a "great peace"? It is infinite peace, *"the peace* ***of God,"*** that is, not only the peace that God gives, but the deep, infinite peace that there is in the heart of God Himself. And it is for any one of you here who wishes it. Your heart may be tempest tossed tonight. Your heart may be a raging sea of doubts, and fears, and anxieties, and unsatisfied desires and passions. But there is peace for you— "great peace," "perfect peace"—*"the peace of God, which passeth all understanding."*

I wonder if there was ever a more tempestuous soul than that of Saul of Tarsus? He breathed an atmosphere of storm, and passion, and hatred. He breathed out (or, to translate more exactly, "breathed in") *"threatening and slaughter against the disciples of the Lord"* (Acts 9:1 ASV). But that stormy soul found such peace in Jesus Christ and through the power of the Holy Spirit whom Jesus Christ bestows upon all those who receive Him, that even in jail at Philippi, at midnight, when his back was torn and bleeding from the stripes he had just received, we find him singing praises to God. (See Acts 16:23–25.) And, later, in prison at Rome, awaiting sentence of death, no ruffle of anxiety or fear disturbs the deep calm of his soul. It was at that time he uttered such words as these, *"Rejoice in the Lord always: and again, I say, Rejoice"* (Philippians 4:4). And a little further on he writes the words I just quoted, *"In nothing be anxious; but in everything by prayer and supplication with thanksgiving let your requests be made known unto God. And the peace of God, which passeth all understanding, shall guard your hearts and your thoughts in Christ Jesus."* And a little further on he says again, *"I have learned, in whatsoever state I am, therein to be content"* (verse 11). And two verses still further on he says, *"I can do all things in him that strengtheneth me"* (verse 13). Yes, everyone can have great peace, abiding peace, abounding peace, never failing peace, *"The peace of God which passeth all understanding"* (verse 7). Jesus said the night before His crucifixion, in His farewell words to His disciples and to all who should become disciples in after years, *"Peace I leave with you;* ***my peace*** *I give unto you: not as the world giveth, give I unto you. Let not your heart be troubled, neither let it be fearful"* (John 14: 27).

III. A Great Position

There is another great thing anyone can have and that is *a great position.* We have a way of thinking that the great positions are only for a very select few. That is a great mistake. The greatest, grandest, and most glorious of all positions is for anyone who will have it. Very few can ever be the President of the United States. Very few can become members of the U.S. Congress. Very few can ever become kings or emperors. But there is a position far higher than that of congressman or senator, or President of the United States, or king or emperor, that is open to any one of us. Turn to John 1:12, and you will find out just what that position is. This is what it says: *"As many as received him, to them gave He the right to become* ***children of God****, even to them that believe on his name"* (ASV). To be a "child of God" is surely to occupy a higher position than to be an earthly president, prince, king, or emperor. What is any earthly monarch to the King of kings and the Lord of lords?

The greatest and most potent monarch of this earth looks like a gnat when compared with the infinite, eternal God, who created all things seen and unseen. The greatest earthly throne is but a toadstool compared with the throne of God. And the position of becoming God's child and God's heir is open to anyone who desires it in his heart.

One day it was my fortune to run by accident upon a real, live king. I was not looking for him, and he certainly was not looking for me. I was coming down the hall of the University at Leipzig all alone, and I saw a man coming up the stairway all alone. I instantly recognized him as the King of Saxony. Of course, I uncovered and bowed as we passed one another, and he bowed back with a smile, very courteously and very pleasantly. And I had met a king—and he had met—what had he met? He had met a free American citizen, but he had met something more than that, he had met a child of God, and to be a child of God is to hold a far higher position than to be a king. And this position is open to anyone who wishes to fill it, "***As many as received him,*** *to them gave He the right to become children of God, even to them that believe on his name.*" Think of it! *Any man or woman can become a child of God.* Yes, any one.

But some of you will decline that great honor. Why? Because you would rather have some disgusting or contemptible sin than to become a child of God. Or you would rather have the silly satisfaction of calling yourself a skeptic and therefore fancying yourself very brainy and an independent thinker, than to become a child of God. Or you are not willing to endure the world's sneers, and you would rather have this fool world's praise, than to be even a child of God. Oh, for what paltry baubles we trade for this great honor of becoming children of God! What pitiable fools we are. I did it for years myself. I thank our wondrous God that He had mercy upon me and patience with me, and at last brought me to my senses.

IV. A Great Hope

There is another great thing that *anyone can have and that is* ***a great hope.*** Paul described this great hope. He said in Titus 1:2, *"In hope of eternal life, which God, t cannot lie, promised"* (ASV). What a hope that is, ***"hope of eternal life"***! The world has nothing to match against that. The very best the world can give cannot last more than eighty, ninety, or a hundred years at the longest. We say this world has been good to Rockefeller. It has given him several hundred millions or it may be a billion. But for how long? For but a very little while. The poorest living newsboy on the streets of this city will be richer than Rockefeller in this world's wealth in a very few years. This world's hopes are poor things, for upon them all is written, "For a few days only."

One day, quite a while ago, the newspapers contained glowing accounts of the magnificent gifts of gold and precious stones presented to two young people who were to be married. The man was the son of one of America's richest millionaires, and the woman, the daughter of another multimillionaire. But in a very few years, they will leave all these costly gifts, all these diamonds and pearls and all this gold. But the one who will believe on Jesus Christ gets a hope that is indeed great: eternal life—life, divine in its quality, endless in its duration, the very life of God Himself. Years roll on, but the life eternal still lasts. Centuries fly by, but the life eternal still lasts. Ages and ages sweep on in endless procession, but the life eternal is just beginning. Ah! Eternal life! That is something worthwhile. To me, there is a growing charm in these words: "eternal life." In former years, I did not think much of them. The present life seemed fair and long and very alluring. But of late years, as I have seen one thing after another end, as I have seen vast fortunes crumble, and one great man after another pass into oblivion and someone else come on and take his place, as I have seen not only vast fortunes but mighty kings and even vast empires collapse and vanish, as I have seen the stamp of transitoriness and decay upon everything earthly, I have felt an ever-increasing pity for the poor fools who live for the present fleeting world, and an increasing joy in these great words, "eternal life."

"In hope of eternal life," that is indeed a hope worth having. And anyone here can have it. The poorest can have it just as well as the richest. The weakest can have it just as well as the strongest. The most sinful can have it just as well as the holiest. The great, the glorious hope of life eternal is open to all.

V. A Great Inheritance

Then there is another great thing that is open to all and that is, *a great inheritance*. Peter describes this inheritance in this way, *"An inheritance* ***incorruptible****, and* ***undefiled****, and that* ***fadeth not away, reserved*** *in heaven"* (1 Peter 1:4). Now that cannot be said about any earthly inheritance. What earthly inheritance is incorruptible? The hand of decay is upon every earthly inheritance. What earthly inheritance is undefiled? My! How dirty most great earthly inheritances are! What earthly inheritance does not fade away? They are fading, every last one. The fool son or grandson of the shrewdest millionaire is likely to wind up in jail, and the inheritance disappears entirely in every case as soon as the owner of it dies.

Paul described this great inheritance that any one of us can get in a still more remarkable way in Romans 8:16–17, *"The Spirit himself beareth witness with our spirit, that we are children of God: and if children, then heirs;* ***heirs of God****, and* ***joint-heirs with Christ****"* (ASV). Think of that a moment please: *"heirs of God"*! Heirs of all God's infinite wealth, joy, and glory, and *"joint-heirs* [fellow heirs, co-heirs] *with Christ,"* heirs in the way in which Jesus Christ is heir and to the extent to which Jesus Christ is an heir. Co-heirs with Him in whom dwelt *"all the fullness of the Godhead bodily"* (Colossians 2:9);

and who was, therefore, the *"heir of all things"* (Hebrews 1:12). In that same way the one who receives Jesus Christ becomes an heir of God. Look out upon the whole earth with all its wealth and say, "This all belongs to God, and I am His child and His heir, and therefore I am heir of all this." Look up at the stars, those great immeasurable, incomprehensible, overwhelmingly stupendous worlds of light and splendor and bewildering magnitude and majesty, and say, "I am an heir of all these." Think of the infinite wisdom, infinite joy, and infinite glory of the Deity, and say, "I am His child. Therefore, all this is my inheritance. There is absolutely no limit to what is open to me." Millionaire? That is nothing. Billionaire? That is still nothing. I am an heir of God, a co-heir with Jesus Christ! It fairly makes one's head swim just to think of it. This inheritance is open to anyone. Take, for example, some washerwoman. This inheritance is open to her. Or some laboring man. This inheritance is open to him. Or an ex-convict. This inheritance is open to him. Or men and women who have squandered their lives. This inheritance is open to them.

One night in Birmingham, England, upon going on to the platform in Bingley Hall, I received a note from a young woman. She asked me to pray for her brother who she said had squandered two fortunes and had just returned from India where he had squandered a third. I read the note from the platform and the audience joined me in prayer for this man. Though we did not know it, miles away in Worcester, while we prayed, that man was seated by a table with a loaded revolver upon it preparing to take his own life. But God heard our prayer, and he was converted and saved as he sat by that table, within just a few minutes of hell. He had thrown away three inheritances, but he received that night an inheritance to which all three together were as nothing.

There are poor men, and there are rich men. There are good men, and there are bad men. But this inheritance is open to one and all without distinction. Listen to the way Peter put it, *"an inheritance incorruptible, and undefiled, and that fadeth not away, reserved in heaven* ***for you***" (1 Peter 1:4). For whom? Listen. *"**For you, who are kept by the power of God through faith** unto a salvation ready to be revealed in the last time"* (verse 5). Do you take in the force of these words? This inheritance is for anyone who believes on Jesus Christ and who, therefore, is kept, not by his own power, but *"by the power of God,"* unto that complete salvation of spirit, soul, and body that is to be made manifest in the last time. That, then, is all one has to do to get this great inheritance: just place faith in Jesus Christ and be *"kept by the power of God through faith unto* [that glorious, infinite] *salvation ready to be revealed in the last time."* Anyone can do that, and therefore anyone can get this inheritance.

We see, then, that there is for us all, for anyone who will have them, a great joy, a great peace, a great position, a great hope, and a great inheritance. Do you want these five great things? I put the question to each one of you. Do you want these five great things? You can have them. Take Jesus Christ as your Savior and surrender to Him as your Lord, and confess Him as such before the world, and these five great things become yours. Do that and you will get them all. Oh, how can any one of you refuse to do it? How can you hesitate to do it? If I would take a bushel basket full of large diamonds of the finest water and make it known that anyone who wished could have one, would you hesitate? There might be some friend near you, to laugh at you, but you would come just the same. Well, I am setting out something infinitely better than a basket full of fine diamonds. I set forth a great peace. I set forth here a great joy. I set forth a great position. I set forth a great honor. I set forth here a great hope. I set forth here a great inheritance. And I say on the authority of God, who cannot lie, "Come up and help yourself." How many of you will?

8

NOAH AND HIS ARK

"And Jehovah said unto Noah,
Come thou and all thy house into the ark."
—Genesis 7:1 ASV

Noah was one of the most remarkable men in the world's history. He stands out absolutely alone of all the men of his day. He was the one man whom God chose out of the whole human race then living to be the head of a new race. The story of the flood is a most amazing one, so unusual indeed that one's first impulse is to question its historicity. But it has abundant confirmation even outside the Bible. Legends of a universal flood are found well-nigh everywhere where men are found. The cuneiform tablets of central Asia, the Bhagavatas of ancient India, the legend of Deucalion in Greece, the traditions of the Cree Indians of North America, and the Orinoco natives in South America, as well as the lore from places as far apart as China, Mexico, Scandinavia, and Ireland all contain accounts of such a flood. The three great branches of the human race—the Turanians,

Semites, and Aryans—all have it. So, it is evident that this extraordinary story of the flood has abundant historic confirmation outside of the very plain and very full and very precise statements of the Bible.

More important, the Old Testament story has the endorsement of Jesus Christ. You cannot doubt the truth of the story of the flood as recorded in the book of Genesis without discrediting Jesus Christ. If this story is not true, Jesus Christ was a fool, for He expressed in the most unmistakable terms His belief in the truth of the story. Yes, if this story is not true, Jesus Christ was worse than a fool. He was a fraud. He claimed to be a teacher sent from God, who spoke the very words of God. If the story of the flood is not true, if it is not accurate history, Jesus accepted an idle tale as true history, and His claim to be a teacher sent from God, who spoke the very words of God, was absolutely false and He was a gross impostor.

Not only the credibility but also the honor of Jesus Christ is involved in the truthfulness and accuracy of this Old Testament story of the flood. But Jesus Christ's claims to have been a teacher sent from God who spoke the very words of God are abundantly substantiated. They are so abundantly substantiated that no one can thoroughly and candidly study the conclusive proofs of the truth of His claims and not believe in them, and consequently he must believe in the truth of the story of the flood that Jesus Christ so explicitly and fully endorsed.

So it is absolutely certain that the story of the flood as recorded in the book of Genesis is true history. It is true that the world was swept in judgment by a flood and Noah and his family, eight persons in all, alone were saved of all members of the Adamic race then living on the earth. Why was Noah saved? The Bible tells us.

I. Noah Was Saved by Grace

Noah was saved because *he found grace in the sight of Jehovah.* God's own statement is, *"Noah found grace in the eyes of the Lord"* (Genesis 6:8). Noah was not saved because he deserved to be saved. He was "saved by grace." He was not saved because he was sinless. It is true that he was *"righteous,"* Genesis 7:1 says so, but it also says that he was *"righteous before God,"* and the only righteousness in God's sight is the righteousness of faith. Hebrews 11:7 tells us that Noah's righteousness was a righteousness of faith and not a righteousness that he worked out for himself. The exact words are, *"Noah…became heir of the righteousness which is by faith."* Noah's righteousness was the kind of righteousness that is open to every one of us, open to the vilest sinner on earth. Noah was a sinner. He was not sinless; he was far from it. He was far from perfect; he got drunk even after the Flood and his wonderful deliverance. (See Genesis 9:21.) Of course, he had more excuse for getting drunk than you or I would have today. He did not understand the effects of alcohol as fully as we do, but he surely must have known that it was not right to get drunk. He was a *sinner saved by grace.* So must we be sinners saved by grace if we are saved at all, and we all can be saved in that way, and not one of us can be saved in any other way. God's Word is as plain as day on that point, and universal experience confirms God's Word at this point. God says, *"There is no difference: for all have sinned, and come short of the glory of God; being* ***justified freely by his grace*** *through the redemption that is in Christ Jesus"* (Romans 3:22–24). And He says again, *"For* ***by grace*** *have ye been saved through faith; and that not of yourselves: it is the gift of God"* (Ephesians 2:8).

II. Noah Was Saved by Faith

Noah was saved because *he believed God.* As God puts it in Hebrews 11:7, *"By faith Noah, being warned of God of things not seen as yet, moved with fear, prepared an ark to the saving of his house."* God told Noah that there was to be a flood, and Noah believed Him. Noah believed that there was to be a flood just because God said so. He had no other reason whatever for believing it; he asked no other reason for believing it. The wisest philosopher on earth is the man who has sense enough to believe what an infinitely wise God, who cannot lie, says, even if he has no other ground for believing it. And there is no bigger fool on earth than the would-be philosopher who doubts anything God says simply because he has no other ground for believing it than God's unsupported Word. The wisest man of his day well said, *"Seest thou a man wise in his own conceit? there is more hope of a fool than of him"* (Proverbs 26:12), and these puny self-styled "philosophers" and would-be "scientists" of our day who are so "wise in their own conceit" that they venture to doubt God's Word because it does not agree with some of their "erudite" notions, would do well to lay this wise utterance of Solomon's to heart.

Jehovah said, "There is to be a flood," and Noah had sense enough to believe it with all his heart just because God said so, and thus *"he condemned the world, and became heir of the righteousness which is by faith"* (Hebrews 11:7). And by his wise action in this matter he not only *"condemned the world"* that then was, but condemned a very large share of the world that now is. Happy is the man today who has as good sense in this matter as Noah had so many centuries ago.

There was no sign of a flood. The sun rose and set year after year just as it always had. The laws of nature moved on in their uniform course. No man of science saw anything indicative of an approaching flood. But God said to Noah, "There is to be a flood," and Noah believed it. People tried to laugh him out of it. They pointed to the steady course of the seasons, the uniformity of nature, to the fact that all of the great scientists were against him, that the theologians and the scholarly critics were all against him, that indeed all kinds of scholars were against him, that in fact he stood entirely alone.

Nevertheless, Noah stuck to his faith in God's Word. Many doubtless said, "Noah, you are mistaken in thinking it is God's Word. It is not God's Word. If it were God's Word our great men would believe it." Some doubtless said that there was no God anyway, and that all this belief in God and God's Word was mere empty superstition.

But Noah believed God in the face of it all, and it was well for him that he did. Unquestionably believing God's Word saved him and his whole family from utter destruction. You and I must be saved in exactly the same way if we are saved at all. We also have God's Word. The proof that this Book is God's Word is overwhelmingly conclusive, and God's Word, as found in this Book, tells of another coming judgment. It tells us that in that judgment many will be eternally lost. God's Word about that is not generally believed. Many men of science do not believe it, and in this day many theological professors do not believe it, and not a few preachers even ridicule the idea. Many scoff at the very idea of God having a Word at all, and some even question whether there is a God. But there is a God, and this Book is God's Word. That can be easily proven. And God's Word says that there is to be a judgment of all mankind (see Acts 17:31), and God's Word about that, just as God's Word about the flood, will be fulfilled to the letter.

Our salvation depends upon our holding fast to God's Word, and believing it to the very letter, in spite of objections and sneers and specious arguments of men, even of scholarly men. Oh, happy is the man who has sense enough to learn from the unvarying history of the past and believe what God says in spite of the proud unbelief of men, no matter who they may be.

III. Noah Was Saved by Obedience

Noah was saved because *he obeyed God. "Jehovah said unto Noah, Come thou and all thy house into the ark"* (Genesis 7:5), and

Noah came and brought all his house with him just as God had bidden him. Noah's faith was a real faith. Noah's faith was not a mere opinion of the head. That sort of faith will not save anyone. Noah's faith was a faith of the heart, a faith that acts upon what it believes, that obeys the God it believes in; and that is the only kind of faith that saves anybody. God said, *"Make thee an ark"* (Genesis 6:14), and told Noah exactly how to make it. Noah made the ark and made it exactly after God's specifications. He attempted no improvements of his own upon God's plans. He was wise enough to do exactly as God told him. The ark God commanded him to build was on a vast scale, and it must have seemed like a huge undertaking. Not only that, it must have seemed like an absurd undertaking. And it was a very expensive undertaking. No doubt Noah was ridiculed. No doubt men tried to dissuade him. No doubt some of his most judicious and trusted friends pointed out more profitable ways to invest his money and more pleasant ways to employ his time, but Noah went right on *doing exactly what God told him to do.*

It is probable that he put all that he had into that old ark. He had nothing to bank on but God's Word, but that was enough. It was well for him that he banked on it. It is always well to bank on God's Word. Very likely it cost Noah his entire fortune to build the ark, and when the last nail was driven, he had nothing left. But when he came out of the ark, he owned the whole earth. It was all his. There were no rival claimants. His title was clear and indisputable. All the men who had laughed at him were dead. They had lost everything. Noah had gained everything. So will it be with you and me, if we obey God. The one who obeys God may lose everything for the time being, but he will gain everything for eternity; for he becomes *"heirs of God, and joint-heirs with Christ"* (Romans 8:17).

God told Noah to build the ark for his own salvation and the salvation of his house. What does God command us to do for our salvation and that of our house? Acts 16:31 answers the question: *"Believe on the Lord Jesus Christ, and thou shalt be saved, and thy house."* God commands us to believe *on* Jesus Christ, not to believe *about* Him, but to believe *on* Him. That means to accept Him, to take Him, to take Him as your Savior, to take Him as your Lord and Master, surrender yourself absolutely to His will, and confess Him as your Lord and Master before the world. (See John 1:12; Romans 10:9–10.) Do that and you shall have life, eternal life. You will be ridiculed if you do. No doubt of that. If some young men who may read these words accept Christ, their companions will make fun of them tomorrow morning. If some businessman accepts and confesses Christ, some of his business friends will make fun of him. If some wives accept Jesus Christ, now their husbands will certainly ridicule them. It may cost any of these a good deal. It may cost some of them their position. It may cost some of them all they have in the world, just as it cost Noah. But it will pay. They will gain more than even Noah did, though he gained the whole earth. They will gain an *"inheritance incorruptible, and undefiled, and that fadeth not away, reserved in heaven for you"* (1 Peter 1:4). They will become heirs of God and joint heirs with Jesus Christ. They may have to suffer with Christ but the old Book of God says, *"If we suffer with him,...we* [shall] *be also glorified with him"* (Romans 8:17 ASV).

When Noah came out of the ark safe and found the whole earth his, I do not think he regretted the ridicule he had endured, nor the money he had expended. And when you who read my words stand before God and all things are yours for all eternity, you will not regret the ridicule you may have endured nor the money you have expended because of your belief in Jesus Christ and your obedience to God. On the other hand, when those who had ridiculed Noah saw the flood arising, they wished they too had invested all in an ark and were safely housed inside. So in the Judgment Day that is surely coming on this old world, those who sneer at the Christian now, and ridicule the Christian now, will wish that they too had invested their all in Jesus Christ. There were no more skeptics when the flood had gotten well to work, and there will be no skeptics or agnostics nor theosophists in the Judgment Day, and there will be a good many of you gentlemen and ladies who will wish you never had been skeptics or agnostics or theosophists or Christian Scientists falsely so-called. I tell you the smart young man who has caught a few of the stock phrases and arguments of modern infidelity, and goes around laughing at preachers and Christians and those who invite him to the church and to Christ, will wish in that day that he had had more sense and had not done it.

IV. Noah Was Saved because He Accepted God's Invitation

Noah was saved because *he accepted God's invitation.* God had said, *"Come thou and all thy house into the ark,"* and Noah just came. It was not merely the invitation that saved Noah, but his own acceptance of the invitation. That is what will decide the matter with each one of us. We are all invited. God says, *"Whosoever will, let him take the water of life freely"* (Revelation 22:17). The Lord Jesus says, *"Him that cometh to me I will in no wise cast out"* (John 6:37). Will you accept the invitation or will you decline it? It is just as true of many today as it was when our Lord said it when He was here upon earth, *"Ye will not come to me that ye may have life"* (John 5:40), and that is the sole reason why they are lost; they won't accept the invitation.

A friend of mine told me a story many years ago. I do not know where he heard it and, of course, I cannot vouch for its truth; but it exactly illustrates my point. He said that a certain rich Christian worker, who wished to illustrate how men are saved by simply accepting the gospel invitation, offered to pay the debts of everyone who came to his office for that purpose. Most men naturally regarded it as a hoax or a trick of some kind and did not go to his office. One man believed it at least enough to try it. He went, and the rich worker paid every penny of his debts. That man was saved from his burden of debt by accepting the invitation. The invitation was for all, but only the one who accepted it received the salvation offered in it. Noah accepted God's invitation to *"Come into the ark"* and was saved, and every one of us who accepts God's invitation to come into Jesus Christ by accepting Him as our personal Savior, surrendering to Him as our Lord, and confessing Him as such before the world, will be saved. Everyone who does not accept God's invitation to come into Christ will be lost. It is up to every one of you to say for yourself whether you will be saved or whether you will be lost, whether you will spend eternity in heaven or whether you will spend eternity in hell. You decide that by your decision whether you will accept God's invitation or decline God's invitation.

Noah accepted the invitation for his family as well as for himself. He took them in with him. The whole family was gathered in. The record reads, *"And Noah went in, and his sons, and his wife, and his sons' wives with him, into the ark"* (Genesis 7:7). It has been said that it speaks well for Noah that in the midst of such prevailing unbelief, Noah's whole household had such faith in the old man that they all accompanied him into the ark. Perhaps it speaks even better for his consistency and integrity and nobility of character that his daughters-in-law had as much confidence in him as his own sons. It is certainly more than can be said of all professed Christian parents today that every member of their household follows them in the acceptance of Christ. I think the Bible plainly indicates that when a man's family does not come along with him, it is somehow the parent's fault. There is some screw loose somewhere in his character or his conduct. He is worldly or overbearing or not strictly truthful or unchristian somewhere, or else he neglects persistent prayer or wise, Spirit-filled personal effort. At all events God is saying, *"Come thou and **all thy house** into the ark,"* and He says in Acts 16:31: *"Believe on the Lord Jesus Christ, and thou shalt be saved, **and thy house.**"* I do not see how any Christian man or woman can rest while even one child is out of the ark. Suppose Noah had found Shem, Ham, or Japheth lacking. Do you not think he would have made a strenuous effort to find him and bring him in?

In the first church of which I was pastor, there were two women who were members of the church. One of these women, a farmer's wife, had a large family of children, but saw to it that every one of them was saved. Several of them became missionaries. At least three of them are missionaries at the present time. The other woman's children were unsaved. The woman who had brought her own children to Christ one by one went to the other woman in a time of deep religious interest and tried to stir her up to win her own children to Christ. But the woman replied, "Oh, I believe they will all be saved—sometime." But they were not. One of them at least is dead now and died out of Christ.

Dr. George Pentecost once talked with a young man whose mother was a professing Christian. The young man sneered at Christianity and at Christians. Dr. Pentecost said to him, "Oh, you think then that Christians are weak in their minds, that they have a soft spot in their brains somewhere, or else they are hypocrites?" The young man replied, "Well, I don't like to put it just that way, but that is about what I think." "But," said Dr. Pentecost, "is not your mother a Christian?" "Yes." "Is your mother weak-minded or is she a hypocrite?" "You have no right to speak that way of my mother," the young man hotly replied. "No, but you said that all Christians had a soft spot in their brains somewhere, and you say your mother is a Christian." The young man blushed, hesitated, and then replied, "If my mother really is a Christian, why then has she never spoken to me about my soul?" That is what some of your children are thinking of some of you professing Christians. Which one of your children are you willing to have lost? Oh, if you have an unsaved child, let God's invitation sink down to the very depths of your heart, *"Come thou, and* ***all thy house*** *into the ark."*

V. Jehovah Shut Him In

Let me call your attention to five wonderfully expressive words in the Bible account of the Flood. They are found in Genesis 7:16, *"And Jehovah shut him in"* (ASV). When God shut to the door of that ark, Noah was safe. The torrential rains might fall from above, the earth might subside beneath, and the waters of the sea might rush in upon the doomed land, but Noah was safe inside the ark built according to God's pattern. And so with us also, when once we are in the ark *built according to God's pattern,* when we are in Christ, by accepting Christ with our whole heart. When we accept Christ fully as our Savior, surrender to Him unreservedly as our Lord, and gladly confess Him as such before the world, God shuts us in and we are safe. There may be appalling storms. There may be fierce tempests. There may be an awful Judgment Day. We may be weak in ourselves, but we are safe. That awful "Great Tribulation" of which the Bible so often speaks and toward which things seem to be so rapidly moving today, in Russia and Germany and England and even in America, may come, but we are safe, "shut in" the ark. And our Lord Jesus Himself said in John 10:28–29: *"I give unto them eternal life; and they shall* ***never*** *perish, and no one shall snatch them out of my hand. My Father, who hath given them unto me, is greater than all; and* ***no one is able to snatch them out of the Father's hand"*** (ASV).

It was not any strength or goodness of his own that made Noah safe in that awful day. It was *being in the ark* that made him safe. It is not any strength or goodness that you or I may have that makes us safe, it is being in Christ Jesus, being in the ark made on God's pattern, thoroughly well built, and that ark will stand any storm.

But the door that shut Noah and his family in also shut the unbelieving world out. When the door was once shut, the day of grace was ended. The door had stood open many years, "*the long-suffering of God* [had] *waited in the days of Noah, while the ark was a preparing*" (1 Peter 3:20). God's long-suffering grace had waited one hundred years and more. But the day of grace was now over. The day of grace will soon be over with you. The door is still open. It will be shut someday. It will be shut for some of you before another year passes. It will be shut for some of you before another month passes. It will be shut for some of you before another week passes. It will be shut for some of you before another day passes. Of course, I do not know who the people are who will read this solemn declaration. But whoever you are, do not presume on God's long-suffering mercy. Listen to the solemn words of Him who proved His love by dying to save you, "*When once the master of the house is risen up, and hath shut to the door, and ye begin to stand without, and to knock at the door, saying, Lord, Lord, open to us; and he shall answer and say to you, I know ye not whence ye are*" (Luke 13:25).

Let us go back in thought to the last day of the antediluvian world. One of the most wonderful paintings I ever saw is Schorn's "The Deluge" in the new Pinakothek in Munich, Germany. The painting is unfinished, but it is a masterpiece. That day broke bright and clear as other days had. There was little sign of any approaching catastrophe. Noah had gone into the ark, the animals had gathered from near and far and gone in too, and the people had been a little startled by this strange procession of animals coming from the four points of the compass. But seven days had gone by since then, and nothing had happened, and their fright had passed away. (See Genesis 7:4–10.) These seven days were seven days of despised mercy. Not only their fear had passed away, so also had their opportunity. Men and women went about their ordinary pursuits again. *"They were eating and drinking, marrying and giving in marriage, until the* [very] *day that Noah entered into the ark"* (Matthew 24:38). Evening came on, and the streets were crowded with people. In many a house, there were decadent festal scenes. The sun went down in a cloud. There were rumblings of distant thunder. Men laugh and say, "This is a striking coincidence. Old Noah said the flood would come today, and really it does look like rain." The more timid are fearful. The rain begins to patter in the streets and people hurry on to their destination. Now the storm bursts in its fury. The heavens are illumined with white and purple light, then, all is dark. The thunder roars and reverberates. The water falls in cloudbursts. The earth seems to be sinking.

It is sinking. It is slowly sinking beneath the level of the sea. The waters of the lake overflow, and the Caspian Sea will soon burst its ancient barriers and flood the entire inhabited earth. Yes! The waters are pouring in now, *"the fountains of the great deep* [are] *broken up"* (Genesis 7:11). Terror-stricken men and women with ashen faces flee from theatres, ballrooms, and homes. To the hills and to the mountains! Still the land is sinking and the waters are rising. The beasts of prey forget their savage instincts and cower beside terror-stricken men and women. Higher and higher rise the waters. Strong men fight with feeble women for the place of vantage. The waters sweep over a low hill and a hundred souls huddled upon it are swept into eternity.

Look! On yonder hill stand a husband and wife alone. The waters are fast coming nearer and nearer. With her former love turned into savage hate, the woman turns on the man she has loved and cries, "Man, you have deceived me, ruined me. I longed to enter the ark and you laughed me out of it." The remorseless waters sweep them away together.

Look again! Yonder is a maiden. She, too, had longed to enter the ark, but none of her friends had gone in, and she was unwilling to go alone. The waters sweep her away on their angry bosom, and soon the fair face sinks beneath the flood. Yonder is a man who had mocked at Noah's faith, but now fear and agony are depicted on the distorted countenance, and now it sinks beneath the flood. A young man who has hesitated long in indecision turns an appealing look toward heaven, but it is too late, and he too sinks beneath the engulfing waters. Thus they go down, singly, by pairs, by hundreds, until the last man of the unbelieving world has disappeared. The end has come. The whole land is submerged, not an unbeliever left, but yonder floats the ark of God in safety while the moon sheds its gentle light upon the unbroken surface of the great deep.

There is another day of doom hurrying on. God tells us in this Book, *"He hath appointed a day, in the which he will judge the world in righteousness by that man whom he hath ordained; whereof he hath given assurance unto all men, in that he hath raised him from the dead"* (Acts 17:31). Are you ready for that day? Come into the ark. Believe God. Obey God. Accept the invitation. Accept Jesus Christ. Confess Him before the world. Let the world laugh if it will. Some of you in the deepest impulses of your heart would like to get right down on your knees now and beg God for mercy. Do it. Don't mind what people say. Don't mind who laughs. "Come into the ark."

9

TIME AND ETERNITY CONTRASTED

"For our light affliction, which is for the moment, worketh for us more and more exceedingly an eternal weight of glory; while we look not at the things which are seen, but at the things which are not seen: for the things which are seen are temporal [for a season]*; but the things which are not seen are eternal* [for eternity]."
—2 Corinthians 4:17–18

The apostle Paul had to endure some things that to most men would seem very hard to bear, and some of these afflictions continued through many years. Indeed the thirty years of his Christian experience seem, at first sight, like thirty years of self-denial and suffering for Christ. But in speaking of these afflictions in our text, Paul spoke of them as "our light afflictions" and also as "our affliction which is for a moment." Is thirty years "but a moment"? Yes, when compared with eternity. Your life of eighty or ninety years or one hundred years is but the twinkling of an eye when compared with eternity. And is the loss of friends, the loss of ease, the loss of the admiration and applause of men, the loss of home and native land, the loss of all that men ordinarily hold dear; and imprisonment and shipwreck and scourging and wandering and hunger and stoning, is all this "light afflictions"? Yes, when compared with the joy and honor and glory that are to be revealed in us in a glad day, which is soon coming. When the sufferings of this present time are put in comparison with the eternal glories that are thus secured, they are nothing at all. And when all the wealth and pleasure and honors that one can possibly get in this world are put in comparison with the eternal agony and ruin and despair and shame that it costs to live for this world, they, too, are nothing. Suppose one gets a million dollars or two million dollars or one hundred million dollars at the cost of being lost forever? Does it pay? Suppose one's whole life from boyhood or girlhood to old age is one constant round of parties, feasts, frolics, and merriments, at the cost of spending an eternity in hell. Does it pay? The truly wise man does not look at the things that are seen, which are "for a time," but at the things that are unseen, which are for eternity. This, then, is really our subject tonight, *eternity*.

I. There Is an Eternity and We Must Go There

The first thing our text teaches us, and which we know to be true even though it were not in our text, is this: *There is an Eternity, and we must go there*. It is the height of folly to refuse to think of eternity. A lady said to me one day, speaking of a certain shiftless young man who has had great opportunities in life but thrown them all away, "He just lives for today; he never thinks of the future either in the life that now is or the life that is to come." Everybody sees that that young man is foolish. I do not think there is any difference of opinion on that point among any of those who know him. But is he really much more of a blockhead than the man or the woman who lives only for the brief days that we spend on this earth, and never thinks of that vast eternity that stretches beyond, and to which we are all hurrying on at express speed? *There is an eternity.* I may live ninety or a hundred years of the life that now is, but I shall certainly live millions and billions and trillions of years in the endless eons of years in the life that is to come. I shall live forever and forever.

Eternity is the important thing. The life that now is, is important only because it determines our eternity. Many a man who is wise enough to look somewhat into the future, asks himself the question, "Where and how shall I spend my middle life, and where and how shall I spend my old age?" A man who is still wiser will ask himself the question, "Where and how shall I spend my eternity?" Have you settled that question? Let me put it to every one of my readers: "Have you settled where and how you will spend eternity?" If you have not, there is really but one sane thing for you to do, and that is to settle the question tonight as to where and how you will spend eternity.

II. Where and How We Shall Spend Eternity Is Settled in the Life That Now Is

The second thing we learn is, *Where and how we shall spend eternity is settled in the life that now is.* The life that now is, is the preparation time, and the only preparation time for the life that is to come. This is the preparation time and the only preparation time for eternity. The boy who has wasted his school days, and failed to make preparation for business life, when he gets into the weary grind of a life that is the inevitable outcome of a wasted boyhood and young manhood, would gladly go back and live his wasted boyhood over again; but he cannot. Much less can any man or woman who wastes this present life on earth come back from a ruined eternity and live this present life over. It cannot be done. You are making your eternity today.

Men have tried to fancy that there is some other time of preparation in the future for those who waste this present opportunity for preparation in the life that now is. Such a hope is the "baseless fabric of a dream," which has not one atom of foundation either in common sense or the more sure Word of God. "If you die in your sins," says Jesus, "*whither I go ye cannot come*" (John 8:21). This word of our Lord Himself makes it as clear as day that where and how we shall spend eternity is settled in the life that now is, settled this side the grave.

You are making your eternity *now*. Some young man or woman may be saying in their heart, "I will go out and have one more fling at sin." Do it, and it may land you in hell for all eternity. In the lost world of endless midnight and despair, you will look up and say, "Dr. Torrey told me that if I went out to spend one more night in sin, I would spend eternity in hell, and here I am." And you will wring your hands, and you will shriek, and you will agonize, and you will despair, but it will be too late, too late forever.

I was dealing one night with a man in Minneapolis who was under deep conviction of sin. I urged upon him immediate acceptance of Jesus Christ, but he hesitated, and he went out without deciding. He thought he would go into a saloon and have one more drink, and he did, and that led to another, and so on. Two years later I received a letter from him from the State Prison at Stillwater, telling me how near he had come to accepting Christ that night, but how he had gone to have another drink and then another, and how he had become intoxicated, and while intoxicated, he had stolen an overcoat and was arrested, tried, and found guilty. He had no recollection of stealing the coat, but said he had no doubt that he did. He was sentenced to two years in Stillwater State Prison. He added, "I have accepted Christ here, but these two years have been wasted, because I did not do as you urged me to that night." But ah, that was not so bad as to wake up in hell and know that you are to spend all eternity there, because you did not take the step that you know you ought to take tonight.

III. How to Secure a Blessed and Glorious Eternity

We have seen that there is an eternity, and we have seen that where and how we shall spend eternity is settled in the life that now is; so we come face to face with the question, *What must I do in the life that now is that I may have a satisfactory and glorious eternity?*

First, if you are to have a satisfactory and glorious eternity, you must believe on Jesus Christ in the life that now is. God tells us this in His Word over and over again. For example, He says in John 3:36, *"He that believeth on the Son hath everlasting life: and he that believeth not the Son shall not see life; but the wrath of God abideth on him."* And He says in Romans 6:23, *"The wages of sin is death; but the gift of God is eternal life through Jesus Christ our Lord."* The first thing to do, then, if we are to have a satisfactory and glorious eternity, indeed the first thing we must do if we are to spend eternity outside of hell, is to believe on the Lord Jesus Christ. Just what does it mean to believe on the Lord Jesus Christ? God Himself answers that question in John 1:12: *"As many as* ***received him****, to them gave he power to become the sons of God, even to them that believe on his name."* Here we are told that to believe on Jesus Christ, to "*believe on his name,*" is to "receive him"; that is, to simply accept Him to be to us what God offers Him to be to everyone, to receive Him as the Savior who has borne our sins for us, borne them in His own body on the cross, and who is therefore ready and able to forgive all our sins as soon as we confess them, and forsake them and put our trust in Him, to receive Him also as our Lord and Master to whom we surrender the entire control of our lives, to receive Him as our divine teacher to whom we surrender our thoughts. Whatever else we may do or not do, it is absolutely sure we shall not have a blessed eternity if we do not thus receive Jesus Christ.

Second, *if we are to have a satisfactory and glorious eternity, we must serve Jesus Christ.* We are saved by grace; but we are rewarded according to our works. Eternity begins with the coming of Christ, and at His coming, Jesus Christ "*shall reward every man* ***according to his works***" (Matthew 16:27). Our eternity will be rich and full just in proportion to the faithfulness of our service here on earth. There are many who fancy that all professed Christians will have an equally glorious eternity, but this is pure fancy. It contradicts the plain teachings of the Word of God, and the teachings of sanctified common sense as well. The Word of God tells us that some will be saved "*so as by fire*" (1 Corinthians 3:15); but that others will have an abundant entrance into "*the everlasting kingdom of our Lord and Savior Jesus Christ*" (2 Peter 1:11). The one who barely accepts Christ, and who holds on to the world in a measure, and does scarcely anything for his Master, will have no such entrance into "*the everlasting kingdom of our Lord and Savior Jesus Christ.*" He will have no such glorious eternity as the one who turns away from the world with his whole heart, and gives up all its follies and self-indulgences and "comes out" and "is separate" (see 2 Corinthians 6:17) and *lives wholly for Christ, a life of constant self-denial and constant service.* Do you realize, you professed Christians, that you are preparing your eternity by the way you serve Christ in the life that now is? Do you realize that your eternity will be richer or poorer by the way in which you serve Jesus Christ on earth? Do you realize that every day spent in hard service will make heaven that much richer and every day and hour frittered away will make heaven that much poorer? Ah, ponder again those familiar words that God spoke to Daniel, *"They that be wise shall shine as the brightness of the firmament; and* ***they that turn many to righteousness*** *as the stars for ever and ever"* (Daniel 12:3). How important then is every day of our Christian life? Let me put to you the question: Has today counted as much as it might have counted for eternity?

Again let me say, that the sufferings we endure, and the sacrifices we make for Christ will make eternity richer. The words of our Lord Jesus are very plain on this point; He says, *"Blessed are ye when men shall reproach you, and persecute you, and say all manner of evil against you falsely for my sake. Rejoice and be exceeding glad: for great is your reward in heaven: for so persecuted they the prophets which were before you"* (Matthew 5:11–12 ASV). There are some who bitterly regret it when they are called upon to be reproached or slandered or in any way to suffer persecution for Jesus Christ's sake. So far from regretting it, we should rather rejoice in it instead. We should be "exceeding glad," these things bring great reward in heaven. Every sneer that one endures, every reproach that is heaped upon us, every loss that we sustain for the sake of the truth and for the sake of the Lord Jesus Christ, brings glorious reward in eternity. Never forget what Paul said: *"For I reckon that the sufferings of this present time are not worthy to be compared with the glory which shall be revealed in us"* (Romans 8:18), and how he says again, "If I suffer, I shall also reign with him." (See 2 Timothy 2:12.) The seemingly awful tortures endured by the Armenian Christians rather than give up their faith in Christ, and which to some people seem so inexplicable, are no longer a mystery if we only bear in mind how they will bring reward a thousandfold throughout all eternity. Do not whine, but thank God every time it is your privilege to suffer for Christ. The more you suffer, the more you should rejoice. The opportunity to suffer for Christ or for the truth is an opportunity for an investment that pays an eternal dividend.

Again, *if we would have a thoroughly satisfactory and glorious eternity, we must use our money for Jesus Christ.* The use we make of our money in the life that now is enriches or impoverishes our eternity. The apostle Paul said in 1 Timothy 6:17–19 ASV, "*Charge them that are rich in this present world, that they be not highminded, nor have their hope set on the uncertainty of riches, but on God, who giveth us richly all things to enjoy; that they do good, that they be rich in good works, that they be ready to distribute, willing to communicate; laying up in store for themselves a good foundation against the time to come, that they may lay hold on the life which is life indeed.*" And the Lord Jesus said in Matthew 6:19–20 ASV, "*Lay not up for yourselves treasures upon the earth, where moth and rust consume, and where thieves break through and steal: but lay up for yourselves treasures in heaven, where neither moth nor rust doth consume, and where thieves do not break through nor steal.*" How few people seem to realize that they are making their eternity by their use of their money here on earth, but it is so. I think some of us will look back with regret from the other world and say, "What a fool I was to invest my money in houses and lands and jewels and luxuries, in gewgaws and trinkets, when I might have invested it so it would be paying me interest today."

Men and women, the greatest practical question that confronts you and me is where shall we spend eternity and how shall we spend eternity? Will you spend eternity in heaven or will you spend eternity in hell? Will you spend it in joy and glory unutterable, or will you spend it in misery and shame unutterable? Time is nothing comparable with eternity. Ten, twenty, eighty years is nothing compared with eternity—eternity—eternity! That is the all-important matter. Where you will spend eternity and how you will spend eternity will be determined by your action in this life;

it may be determined, it will be in a measure determined by your action today. What you do today is of tremendous importance. If you have not already accepted Christ, accept Him now. And even if you have accepted Christ, but have been serving Him in a half-hearted way, give yourself up wholly to Him from this time henceforward. If you have been holding back from sacrificing for Christ, make the sacrifice at once. I desire with all my heart that my eternity be just as rich, just as full, just as glorious as possible, and by God's grace I am going to make it so, whatever it costs.

10

ETERNAL LIFE OR THE WRATH OF GOD?

"He that believeth on the Son hath everlasting life: and he that believeth not the Son shall not see life; but the wrath of God abideth on him."
—John 3:36

We have in these words of God a most vivid contrast. I know of no verse in the Bible that is more full of glory in the first part of it and more full of darkest despair in the last part of it. It presents God's alternative, an alternative open to all: *"eternal life"* for all those who believe on the Son, *"the wrath of God"* for those who refuse to believe Him. It leaves each one of us to choose which we shall have.

One of the most meaningful and glorious phrases that was ever uttered is one that was so often upon the lips of our Lord Jesus Christ, *"eternal life"*; one of the most awful and appalling phrases ever uttered is the other phrase that occurs in our text, *"the wrath of God."* It cannot be put into words. It cannot be even conceived in fancy. The wealth of glory there is wrapped up in those two words "*eternal life*." Nor can the depth of dishonor, horror, shame, woe, and despair, that is wrapped up in that other phrase "*the wrath of God*" be put into words, nor can it be conceived by human imagination. It is between these two, the unutterably glorious "*eternal life*" and the immeasurably and unspeakably awful "*wrath of God*," that each of us tonight is called to make his choice: "*He that believeth on the Son hath everlasting life: and he that believeth not the Son shall not see life; but the wrath of God abideth on him.*"

The question then that confronts each of us in this place tonight is this: eternal life or the wrath of God?

Which shall it be? Which shall I choose? That should not be a difficult question to settle. If any man is not a hopeless fool or an utter maniac, he will certainly say, "Give me eternal life: as for the wrath of God, Jesus, Son of God, save me from that." But that is not the choice that some of you who are here tonight are really making. You are deliberately turning your backs on eternal life, and you have been turning your backs on eternal life for years. Some of you are deliberately choosing the wrath of God, and you have been choosing the wrath of God for years. How can we doubt the existence of a personal devil of great cunning and great power when we see how men are so utterly blinded and deceived by his cunning and so completely enslaved mentally by his power, that they choose the wrath of God rather than eternal life? The existence of such a devil as the Bible presents is the only rational explanation of this indubitable fact. You question the existence of a personal devil, yet you yourselves are living demonstrations of his existence and of his marvelous cunning and his exceedingly great power.

I. The Things Contrasted

Now let us look more closely at the two possibilities that are put in such vivid contrast. We cannot possibly conceive the glory of the one or the horror of the other, but we can get some hint of what they mean.

1. What is *"eternal life"*?

(A.) *Eternal life is real life.* In 1 Timothy 6:19, Paul said, *"Lay hold on eternal life."* The Revised Version translates this differently. It reads, *"Lay hold on the life which is **life indeed**."* The Revised Version gives the correct translation, and that is what eternal life is: *"life indeed"*; life not merely in seeming but life in reality. Much that we call life is not really life at all, but death. Many a young man or woman plunges into a life of gaiety, worldliness, and sin, and cries as he does it, "I am going to see life for myself." No, you are not going to see life; you are going to see death. Paul was right when he said, *"She that liveth in pleasure is dead while she liveth"* (1 Timothy 5:6). It was really God who said it, God speaking through Paul. It is not life that you see in the saloon with its carousals; it is death. It is not life that you see in the gambling hell with its strange fascination and intense excitement; it is death. It is not life that you see in the theater with its appeal to your lust and your impure fancy, with its many times married actresses, with their fair faces and foul hearts, and with its actors who are so often the wreckers of happy homes; it is death. It is not life that you see in the movies with their constant appeal to all that is lowest and vilest in men and women; it is death. It is not life that you see in the ballroom where supposedly decent women permit a familiarity of approach and contact that is nowhere else permitted except by the most indecent women; it is death. It is not life that you see in the costly receptions of the rich with their vain display of jewels and fine apparel, and with their so frequently disgusting and shocking immodesty in dress; it is death. Anywhere and everywhere a life of sin is death. A life of selfishness is death. A life of pleasure is death. (See 1 Timothy 5:6.) A life of worldliness is death. It is not life; it is death. But *"eternal life"* really is life. It is *"life indeed."* It deserves the name life, and no one really knows what life is who has not received eternal life through Jesus Christ our Lord. Eternal life is life indeed.

(B.) *Eternal life is fullness of life.* It is life abundant. Jesus once said, "*I came that they may have life, and may* ***have it abundantly***" (John 10:10 RV). Eternal life is life full of beauty, full of peace, full of joy, full of power, full of glory, abundant life, abounding life, overflowing life.

(C.) *Eternal life is satisfying life.* No life but eternal life can ever satisfy the longing and capacity of these souls of ours made in the likeness of God. No life that is purely earthly, no life that we inherit from our ancestors, no matter how fine they may have been and how refined in character, no life but the life we derive directly from God when we receive the Lord Jesus Christ, no life but eternal life can satisfy the infinite yearnings of these spirits of ours made originally in the image of God, and that still in the most depraved of us in their infinite longings retain traces of that divine image in which we were made. "Give me wealth," one man cries, "and I shall be satisfied." "Give me power," another cries, "and I shall be satisfied." "Give me pleasure," another cries, "and I shall be satisfied." "Give me fame," another cries, "and I shall be satisfied." No, you will not be satisfied with any of these nor with all of these. You would far better cry, "Give me God, and I shall be satisfied. Give me eternal life, and I shall be satisfied." Oh! How many I have known to whom this world seemed to have given all that it had to give—but they were not satisfied. And how many I have known to whom this world had given very little of all it has to give, and yet they were satisfied; for they had God and they had eternal life.

(D.) *Eternal life is life of highest knowledge.* Our Lord brings that out in a wonderful way in an utterance that He made at one of the supreme moments of His life, in His prayer with His disciples the night before His crucifixion. When He lifted up His eyes to heaven and spoke to the Father, He said, "*This is eternal life,* ***that they should know thee*** *the only true God, and him whom thou didst send, even Jesus Christ*" (John 17:3 RV). *Eternal life is full knowledge of the infinite.* The knowledge the most erudite scholar has gathered from books, the knowledge the profoundest philosopher has reasoned out for himself in his reasonings, the knowledge the most brilliant scientist has discovered as he studied the rocks beneath his feet or the stars above his head, is nothing to the knowledge that the humblest man or woman obtains who enters into eternal life, knowledge of God, full knowledge of the infinite.

(E.) *Eternal life is perfect life, completeness of life.* It is life in its perfection, in its completeness. All other life than the eternal life that we receive when we receive Jesus Christ is partial, fragmentary, unsymmetrical, unbalanced, incomplete. "*Eternal life*" *is life perfected, filled out, symmetrical, perfectly balanced, complete.* We have a suggestion of this in the words of Paul to Timothy in 2 Timothy 3:15–17 ASV where he said, "*From a babe thou hast known the sacred writings* ["*holy scriptures*" KJV] *which are able to make thee* ***wise unto salvation*** *through faith which is in Christ Jesus. Every scripture given by inspiration of God, and is profitable for teaching, for reproof, for correction, for instruction which is in righteousness. That the man of God may be* ***complete,*** *furnished completely unto every good work.*" Here we see that a saving knowledge of Jesus Christ comes through the written Word, and thus eternal life comes through the Word, as John put it in John 20:31, "*These are* ***written,*** *that ye might believe that Jesus is the Christ, the Son of God; and that believing ye might have life through his name.*" And we further see that by receiving the eternal life through the Word, a man becomes "complete," obtains *complete life,* eternal life.

(F.) *Eternal life is divine life, the very life of God imparted to us.* The apostle John said in his first epistle, the first chapter and the second verse, "*And the life was manifested* [that is, manifested in the person of Jesus Christ], *and we have seen, and bear witness, and declare unto you the life,* ***the eternal life, which was with the Father,*** *and was manifested unto us*" (ASV). Eternal life then is the life of the infinitely holy and blessed God, the infinite life, imparted to us. Oh! It is wonderful, it is amazing! Think of it, that it is your privilege and my privilege, the privilege of me, a poor sinner, an ignoramus, a worm of the dust, one whose heart was once set upon the silly follies of the world and revolting sin, to have the life of the blessed God, the very life of God Himself, mind you, this infinite life, imparted to me!

(G.) *Eternal life is endless life.* Endlessness is not the most essential characteristic of eternal life—its quality is more than its duration—but nevertheless it is endless. I thank God it is. I thank God that He offers me a life that is not only infinite in its quality but endless in its duration. I cannot be satisfied with anything that ever comes to an end. I love flowers. I look in joy upon the little daisy in the grass, on the pansy with its happy, sweetly speaking face, upon the lily of the valley, in its modesty and purity and matchless beauty, to me the dearest of all flowers, upon the rose in its rich, superb splendor; but, as I look upon an exquisite bunch of roses, sadness steals over me for I cannot but think how soon they will fade. "Leaf by leaf, the roses fall; drop by drop, the springs run dry." I love nature, especially the glorious beauty of a sunset in the mountains or by the sea. But as I look at the green and the crimson, the azure, and the gold, and it seems as if the very gates of heaven were about to swing open, it all fades, and it is night and I am chilled and lonely. I love high and noble and ennobling human friendships (in which I have been particularly favored by God); but a few years pass and they are broken by separation or by death and it is all over, and nothing but a memory and a heartache remain.

So it is with everything of earth: it ends. Thank God for something that never ends, something that always has in it the freshness of the dawn, something that ever stretches on and on and on into the illimitable spaces of ever-increasing glory before you. Thank God for *"everlasting life."* Such then is eternal life, real life, fullness of life, satisfying life, life of highest knowledge, complete life, the life of God imparted to us, and life that never ends. Do you not desire it? Do you not desire it with an intensity that will not take "No" for an answer? I do. I would, if necessary, sacrifice everything I hold dear on earth to obtain it, and still think I had made a good bargain, even if it were to cost me the sacrifice of everything that men hold dear on earth. Thank God, eternal life is mine! It is mine! It is mine! I have it now. I already have it in its beginnings, and I have the sure promise of its fullness. I shall never lose it. (See John 10:28–29.) Will you have it too?

2. What is *"the wrath of God"*?

It is just what the words express. I have given a good deal of study to the etymology and the usage of the Greek word that is rendered *"wrath"* in this verse. *It means the intense and settled displeasure of God,* the intense displeasure of that infinitely Holy Being who created us and all things, and who has the absolute control of all the powers and forces of the universe. Every true and wise husband dreads the displeasure of his wife; that is, he would not do anything to incur her displeasure if it could be avoided. Every true and wise citizen dreads the displeasure of his government. Every true son dreads the displeasure of his father. But how much more will every man of understanding and of character dread *"the wrath **of God**."* The wrath of God! There is nothing more awful than that. To have the infinitely Holy One displeased with you; to have the Holy Being, before whom the seraphim veil their faces and cry, *"Holy, holy, holy, is the Lord God Almighty"* (Isaiah 6:3; Revelation 4:8), displeased with you; to have the omnipotent and infinite ruler of the universe displeased with you; to have the mighty One who holds the sun, moon, and stars, and all the myriad systems of worlds of light that stud the illimitable expanse of heaven, in the hollow of His hand, as they move through space with incredible momentum displeased with you; to have the infinitely wise ruler and shaper of the whole history of this tiny ball that we call the earth displeased with you; yes, to have God displeased with you, to incur His wrath, His intense, deep-seated settled displeasure, that is awful! That is appalling! But that is certainly what stares in the face tonight many a man and many a woman in this audience. "*The wrath of God.*" Gather your thoughts together. Think of it! Will you have it? Will you choose it?

Here then there are before you the two alternatives. On the one hand, eternal life, real life, fullness of life, satisfying life, life of highest knowledge, complete life, the life of God, never-ending life, blessedness, and glory, *Eternal life*. On the other hand, the wrath of God, the intense, deep-seated, settled displeasure of the All Holy One, the Maker and Governor of the Universe. Which will you choose? If you choose the latter, someday you will be among those who are described as saying "*to the mountains and to the rocks, Fall on us, and hide us from the face of him that sitteth on the throne and* ***from the wrath*** *of the Lamb: for* ***the great day of their wrath is come****; and who shall be able to stand?*" (Revelation 6:16–17).

II. How One Determines Whether Eternal Life or the Wrath of God Shall Be His Portion

Now we come to the question, and it is a tremendously important question, By what act do we determine whether eternal life or the wrath of God is to be our portion? Listen to God's own answer to this immensely important question. It is not the answer of all modern philosophers. It is not the answer of all modern theologians. It is not the answer of all modern preachers. *But it is God's answer,* and therefore it is true. You will find that answer in the words of our text, "***he that believeth on the Son*** *hath eternal life; and* ***he that believeth not*** *the Son shall not see life; but the wrath of God abideth on him.*" Nothing could be plainer or simpler or more unmistakable than this answer. The one and only act by which we get eternal life is *the act of believing on the Son of God,* believing on Jesus Christ. The one and only act by which we lose eternal life and bring upon ourselves the abiding wrath of God is by refusing to believe on Jesus Christ.

Whosoever believes on Jesus Christ gets eternal life. There it stands in God's sure Word in language a child can understand, "*he that believeth on the Son hath eternal life,*" irrespective of who he is or what he is, irrespective of what he has been or what he has done. He may be a millionaire or he may be a pauper. He may be a scholar or he may be unable to read or write. He may be moral and upright and clean. Or he may be immoral and dishonest and vile, but the moment any man or woman or child believes on the Son, believes on Jesus Christ, the moment that person gets eternal life, they get the actual experience of the beginnings of it, and the fullness that awaits them in the world to come is assured. Any man, any woman, may get eternal life right now. You may get eternal life before you read another page in this book if you desire to do so, and you can have that perfect assurance that comes from knowing that you have God's own Word backing you when you say it.

But what is it to believe on the Son of God? It is to accept God's testimony about Jesus Christ, that Jesus is the Christ, the Son of God, and to act upon that testimony by putting your full and absolute confidence in Him who is so entirely worthy of your confidence, and therefore accepting Him to be to yourselves all that He offers Himself to be: your crucified Savior, who bore every one of your sins in His own body on the cross and thus settled them; your risen Savior who has all power in heaven and on earth, and is therefore able to keep you day by day; and your absolute

Lord and Master, to whom you surrender the entire control of your thoughts and life. *Believing on the Lord Jesus Christ is putting your confidence in Him.* It leads you to entrust to Him your salvation, and to entrust to Him your whole self. Believing on the Son of God will lead you to go right to Jesus Christ, the Son of God, and say to Him, "Lord Jesus, I believe God's testimony about You, that You are God's Son, and that You bore my sins in Your own body on the cross, and that You rose again and are a living Savior today, and I commit myself to You to save, and keep and guide and teach and govern, to do what You will with me. I put my trust in You to save me from the guilt of sin by Your atoning death. I put my trust in You to save me from the power of sin day by day by Your resurrection power. I surrender to You the entire control of my life and thoughts." It is this unreserved committal of yourself to Jesus Christ that brings eternal life, and when you make it you can say with Paul, *"I know whom I have believed, and am persuaded that he is able to keep that which I have committed unto him against that day"* (2 Timothy 1:12).

Will you take that decisive step? You have every reason for believing on the Son of God. The testimony that He really is the Son of God, God's own testimony to that fact, is unanswerable. Will you yield to the testimony and believe on Him?

Now what is the act by which we bring upon ourselves the wrath of God? Oh! The answer to that is so plain. Here it is: *"He that **believeth not the Son** shall not see life; but the wrath of God abideth on him."* The Revised Version renders it, *"he that **obeyeth** not the Son shall not see life, but the wrath of God abideth on him."* The truth is in both the Authorized and the Revised, but neither the Authorized nor the Revised give the exact force of the word that is translated *"believeth not"* in the one case, and *"obeyeth not"* in the other. The word so translated means to *refuse to be persuaded*, or *to refuse to believe*, so exactly translated it would be, *"but he that* *refuseth to believe* [or, disbelieveth] *the Son shall not see life but the wrath of God abideth on him.*" The thought is that those who have heard of Him and do not believe are responsible for not believing, for they have refused to be persuaded by the evidence. They have refused to yield to the evidence. They have refused to believe. That is the exact truth about everyone who goes on without believing on the Son of God, without putting their confidence in the Son of God, without accepting the Son of God as their Savior, their Lord, and their King.

You have had abundant evidence that He is the Son of God. You have had abundant evidence that He can save from the guilt and power of sin, but through love of the world or love of sin or fear of man or for some other reason, you refuse to believe, *you will not believe* on the Son. Well, if you will not believe on the Son of God, Jesus Christ our Lord, if you continue to refuse to yield to the evidence that Jesus is the Christ, the Son of God, with that real faith that leads to obedience to His Word and trust in Himself, you will not get eternal life. No, not only that, but you will get "the wrath of God."

Do you believe Jesus Christ? Do you believe Him with that real faith that leads you to act upon what He says, with that faith that leads you to put your unhesitating confidence in His promises, and to yield unquestioning obedience to His commands, and to put your confidence in Himself? If not, "*the wrath of God abideth upon*" you. It makes absolutely no difference who or what you are. You may not be a criminal. You may not be a moral monster. You may not be low and selfish and dishonest. You may not be contemptible and mean. You may be refined. You may be cultivated. You may be highly cultured. You may be a university student or university professor. You may be amiable. You may be gentlemanly or ladylike. You may be true and kind and generous. But if you do not believe on the Son of God, if you refuse to be persuaded by His words and to put confidence in Himself as your atoning Savior, your risen Savior, to obey Him, if you are not ready to act upon His every word, *"the **wrath of God** abideth upon"* you. The wrath of God—the deep, settled, intense displeasure of God—is resting upon every man and woman, young and old, who does not put confidence in Jesus Christ as the Christ, the Son of God, and stand ready to act upon His every word. *"He that believeth not the Son shall not see life; but the wrath of God abideth on him."* Oh! It is awful! Awful! Awful!

If we could represent God's wrath by a black thunder cloud, and could see things as they really are, we would see a blacker storm cloud than human eye ever beheld hanging over the head of many a man and many a woman in this audience tonight, ready to break. I have been an eyewitness of some terrific storms on sea and land. I was once in a house that was struck by lightning, and at another time I was standing in the door of another house when the lightning struck and splintered a great oak a few feet away, and a part of the lightning passed through the very door where I was standing. One summer at Northfield, I had to go out into an electric storm to quiet a horse that was trembling like a leaf, and take him from underneath a tree, and the lightning in a short time struck three times within sight of where I stood.

But I had a dream one night far more terrible than anything I ever saw in life. It was more than twenty years ago, but I remember it vividly even now, and the appalling horror that swept over me in the midst of the dream. Enormous bags of black, smoke-like, cyclonic clouds with ragged edges rolled up full of wind and electricity, and every moment I expected to see one burst and shoot down with deafening reverberation awful death upon my poor devoted head. That awful dream that made my blood fairly run cold even in my sleep is, I believe, only a faint picture of every man and woman in this house tonight who is out of Christ. *"The wrath of God abideth upon"* you. That awful storm cloud full of lightning, thunder, death, shame, woe, and despair hangs over your head tonight, ready to burst. But God is long-suffering and merciful, He is *"not willing that any should perish"* (2 Peter 3:9), and holds back the execution of His long pent-up wrath. No, even more, He offers you eternal life, real life, fullness of life, perfectly satisfying life, life of highest knowledge, complete life, His own life, endless life, infinite life, life of measureless joy and beauty and power and glory instead. Which will you have, eternal life or the wrath of God? Do I hear someone mutter, "I do not like that kind of preaching. I do not believe it." Then you are giving the lie to God; for it is not I, *it is God who says, "He that believeth on the Son hath everlasting life: and he that believeth not the Son shall not see life; but the wrath of God abideth on him."* Oh! Men and women, there are two possibilities open before you tonight, one infinitely glorious, the other inconceivably appalling. Eternal life or the wrath of God, which will you take?

11

A PERFECT CURE FOR POVERTY AND ALL OTHER EVILS OF THE DAY

"Come unto me, all ye that labour and are heavy laden, and I will give you rest. Take my yoke upon you, and learn of me; for I am meek and lowly in heart: and ye shall find rest unto your souls. For my yoke is easy and my burden is light."
—Matthew 11:28–30

Human life is full of evils; poverty, sickness, bereavement, failure, bitterness of heart, despair, death. If we could see all the tears that have been shed in America today, hear all the sighs and groans and wails and shrieks that have been uttered, witness the heartbreak and despair that have found no visible or audible expression, we would believe in hell. Not in a hell lying beyond the grave, but a hell existing right here and just now. That might make it easier for us to believe in a hell hereafter.

But is there no cure? Must this all go on and on forever? No! It need not go on. *There is a perfect cure for all the ills that man is heir to. There is a cure that is sovereign, sufficient, sure, and speedy.* Jesus Christ announced that cure nearly nineteen hundred years ago, but the overwhelming majority of men and women have not listened, and so our evils, miseries, and despair continue. You will find this cure that our Lord Jesus Christ proposed for all our ills in Matthew 11:28–30, "*Come unto me, all ye that labour and are heavy laden, and I will give you rest. Take my yoke upon you, and learn of me; for I am meek and lowly in heart: and ye shall find rest unto your souls. For my yoke is easy and my burden is light.*" *Christ Jesus Himself is the cure for all our evils.* He came to "*destroy the works of the devil*" (1 John 3:8). He does it for all who receive Him. Poverty, sickness, bereavement, failure, bitterness of heart, despair, and death, as well as sin and unbelief, are all works of the devil, and we can be done with them by coming to Jesus, the Christ of God.

I propose to take up these various evils and show how Jesus, the Christ of God, is the Cure for them all and how each one of us may be done with them right now.

I. Christ Jesus Is the Cure for Sin

*We begin with the greatest of all evils, **sin**.* Men tell us poverty is an evil, and I believe it. They tell us sickness is an evil, and I believe that too. But the monster evil, the evil that lies at the root of all other evils, is sin. Sin is the first great evil to be gotten rid of. The preachers of the so-called "social gospel," and all these philanthropists who are trying to lift men out of their miseries while leaving them in their sins, mean well, but they are attempting the impossible, and must meet finally with utter disappointment. It is like trying to rid men of some sickness by attacking the symptoms and not going to the root of the disease itself. It is like trying to cure smallpox by merely painting the pustules. Sin is the radical evil, the root evil, so we begin there tonight, and that is where we all need to begin in our own lives. *Christ Jesus is the cure for sin.*

1. *Christ Jesus is the cure for sin in the individual.* He is the cure for sin in every individual who will take the remedy.

First, *Christ Jesus saves from the guilt of sin.* Sin cuts men off from God. God is infinitely holy, and so sin makes a great gulf between us and the Holy Being who rules this universe, the Being whom we call God, the only Being who is worthy to be called God. Separated from God, cast off from His grace and power, it is impossible for us to fight sin in our own strength. But Jesus Christ removes the barrier between us and God. He takes our guilt upon Himself and therefore as soon as we take Him as our Sin-bearer, we have again perfect access to God and to His strengthening, delivering, and transforming grace. We read in Galatians 3:13, *"Christ redeemed us from the curse of the law, having become a curse for us: for it is written, Cursed is every one that hangeth on a tree"* (ASV). And we read again in 2 Corinthians 5:21, *"Him who knew no sin, he* [that is, God] *made to be sin on our behalf; that we might become the righteousness of God in him"* (ASV).

One day, some years ago, I heard a man who was brought up in childhood as a thief, who had spent years in prison in various states in the Union, and also in other lands, but who had been brought to see that God loved him vile as he was, and that Jesus had died for him, tell the story how faith in this Christ, Christ Jesus, had opened to him the way to God and to salvation. Thousands upon thousands could tell essentially similar stories. Christ Jesus is beyond question, on the testimony of countless, competent witnesses, a cure for the guilt of sin.

This last week, I was standing on the street waiting for a car, and a man stepped up to me and began to talk to me, and I thought at first he was going to talk about the common subjects of the day, as so many do. But instead of that he at once asked, "Do you think a man can sin away the day of grace?" I looked into his face and into the depths of his eyes, yes, into the depths of his soul. I saw the anxiety and sorrow that were in his heart, and asked him, "Why do you ask?" Then he opened his breaking heart to me right there on the street, and I was able to speak to him of our glorious gospel, how according to it, all our sins had been laid on Jesus Christ and settled, how Jesus had said, *"Him that cometh to me I will in no wise cast out"* (John 6:37). A new light and a new hope came into the man's eyes, and when I left him to take the car there was a smile of peace upon his face. ***There is no other gospel than the gospel of Christ who was crucified for our sins*** *that will bring to a man a profound sense of sins forgiven,* and make him know that no matter how many or how great his sins may have been, there is pardon for him on the ground of the atoning death of Jesus Christ, and that on that single but all sufficient ground he has access to God.

But the Lord Jesus Christ saves not only from the guilt of sin, He also saves from the power of sin. This man of whom I spoke a few moments ago as having been brought up in childhood as a thief, who had spent years in prison in this country and other lands, told of the desperate struggles he had made to break away from the power of sin and to be a man. But failure followed failure, and despair stared the man in the face. Then he took Jesus Christ as his personal Savior, and the fetters of sin, the fetters of the appetite for drink, the fetters of impurity and profanity, and a host of evil habits were snapped in a moment.

This is merely one case in thousands. Christ is a sure cure for sin, a sure deliverer from the power of sin, no matter how deep-seated and desperate the case may be. We read in 1 Timothy 1:15: *"This is a faithful saying, and worthy of all acceptation, that Christ Jesus came into the world to save sinners"*; then Paul added his own experience, *"of whom I am chief."* This statement of Paul's was true, of course. Every statement in the Bible is true, but this particular statement that Jesus Christ came to save the chief of sinners, if he will only put his trust in Him, I have seen verified in countless instances. One morning in the People's Church in Minneapolis, of which I was then pastor, at the close of the morning service, one of my deacons stepped up to a gentleman and said, "Are you a Christian?" "No, sir," he replied. "Why not?" the deacon asked. "I am too great a sinner to be saved," was the reply. To his amazement the deacon exclaimed, "Thank God!" Then the deacon turned to me on the platform and called, "Brother Torrey, here is a man who says he is too great a sinner to be saved. Thank God!" The gentleman looked more bewildered than ever. I stepped down to him and asked, "Is what the deacon says true?" "Yes," he said, "I am too great a sinner to be saved." Though he had the appearance of a gentleman, he was a great sinner. He had run away and left his wife in Toronto, Canada, and was squandering his manhood and his money in gambling in Minneapolis, Minnesota. He had lost thirty-five thousand dollars at the gaming table just the week before.

When he said "I am too great a sinner to be saved," I said, "Let me show you something," and opening my Bible to 1 Timothy 1:15, I asked him to read. And he read, *"This is a faithful saying, and worthy of all acceptation, that Christ Jesus came into the world to save sinners; of whom I am chief."*

"Well," he said "I am chief."

"Well," I said, "then it means you."

"It is a precious promise," he said.

"Will you accept it now?" I asked.

"I will."

I said, "Let us kneel down and tell God so."

We knelt side by side and prayed, and when he arose, he knew that God had forgiven all his sins. He left the following week for the Northwest, and I lost sight of him for nearly a year, for he never wrote me. Then I learned that he had returned to St. Paul and was working every night for the salvation of others, that he had brought his wife from Toronto, that they were reunited and so happy in their new life that they had adopted a little girl from an orphanage to make their home complete.

No man needs to continue in sin. God has provided a cure. The Lord Jesus Himself told us what that cure is in John 8:36, *"If the Son* [that is, the Son of God, Jesus Himself] *therefore shall make you free, ye shall be free indeed."*

2. *Christ Jesus is not only the cure for sin in the individual. He is the cure for sin in society as a whole.*

Men propose various remedies for the cure of sin and crime in the world. The best of them will prove only partially availing. Whatever prohibition laws may affect, they will never banish sin or crime. I believe in prohibition. I believe it was a good thing, a great thing in many ways, as many of us know by personal observation and experience, when the prohibition enactment went into effect in this land. But prohibition does not banish sin, and it never will. There has been more sin and crime in our country since the adoption of prohibition than before. Prohibition is not to blame for that. There are numerous causes, prominent among which is the fact that we are reaping the aftermath of the war. Oh! War is a hellish thing, a most damnable thing. Crime would have been even worse, far worse than it is, if it had not been for prohibition. But while prohibition is not to blame for the increase of sin and crime, the increase of sin and crime after the adoption of prohibition does show that prohibition will not cure sin. Neither will any other kind of external law, no matter how wise and beneficent the law may be, cure sin. Jesus Christ alone, the personal Jesus Christ, is the cure for sin in the individual and also the cure for sin and crime in the state, in the home, and in society in general. It is His coming again that will utterly banish sin and crime from the earth, so that righteousness and the knowledge of the Lord shall cover the earth as the waters cover the sea. (See Isaiah 11:9.)

Jesus then is the cure for all sin in every aspect of its working.

II. Christ Jesus Is the Cure for Unbelief

The next greatest evil to sin is unbelief. Indeed, the two go hand in hand: where sin reigns, unbelief reigns; where unbelief reigns, sin reigns. Unbelief begets sin, and sin fosters further unbelief. Undermine the faith of men in the Bible and in the God of the Bible, and in the Christ of the Bible, and a carnival of lust, greed, passion, hate, dishonesty, murder, and war, with all its accompanying horrors, is the result. Increasing unbelief is one of the chief causes, the one fundamental cause, of the carnival of lust, crime, immorality, immodesty, indecency, lawlessness, banditry, and murder that is sweeping over our land today. Our schools and colleges and universities have been undermining faith in the Bible and in the God of the Bible and in the Christ of the Bible, and we are reaping the harvest; and an awful harvest it is.

The things I read in the papers about men and women being held up and robbed every night, and sometimes murdered, are depressing, but to a man who looks ahead with a clear eye, they are not as depressing as what one sees on every hand of the immodest, bold, shameless conduct of the rising generation, our high-school boys and girls, yes, our grammar-school boys and girls. Unbelief has come into our schools and homes like a flood, and multitudes of our boys and girls instead of being found in Sunday school on the Lord's Day studying the one book of all other books that makes for noble character and good citizenship are found off spending the weekend in the mountains, boys and girls together, and down at the seashore watching and joining in immodest parades and various other things, and are also found in the movies by the thousands, movies whose chief attraction oftentimes is indecency.

Take any daily paper and you will find that it advertises indecent movies with grossly suggestive pictures to allure the young, advertisements of such a character that not so many years ago a paper would have been prosecuted if it had dared to publish them. Even the YWCA, which is supposed to be a Christian institution and "an arm of the church," takes off hiking parties of young girls on the Lord's Day, takes them away from home and Sunday school and church to spend the weekend in a canyon. A further spread of infidelism in our city would bring more profit to the bootleggers, gambling hells, and brothels than a governmental subsidy. But men say, "That may be so, but I cannot help my unbelief. If I cannot believe, I cannot, and that is all there is to it." No, that is not all there is to it. *There is a cure, a sure cure for unbelief. The cure is Jesus Christ.* Go to Christ Jesus. Tell Him your unbelief. Make a clean breast of it. Tell Him you cannot believe in the Bible, that you cannot believe in God, that you cannot believe in Him, the way Christians claim to believe in Him; but, tell Him also, that if the Bible is true, you want to know it, that if there is a God, you want to know it, and want to know Him, and that if He is Himself the Son of God, you want to know that too, and that if He will show you it, you will accept Him as your Savior, and surrender to Him as your Lord, and confess Him as such before the world. Then take the words of Jesus as they have been recorded in the four Gospels. Take in particular the gospel of John and read it honestly, looking for light, and obeying the light just as fast as you get it, and your skepticism and your unbelief will soon vanish. My friend, you may not be to blame for your unbelief; but you will be to blame if you continue in it, for I have pointed out a cure. Thousands have tried this cure. It has never failed in one single instance.

For years I stood in the pulpit of the Moody Church in Chicago and challenged unbelievers to come to me and I would show them a rational cure for their unbelief, and if it did not succeed in any case I would let the unbeliever speak from that platform. Many came, but there was never a case of failure, not a single one where men really took the remedy suggested. One night a man was brought to me. He had boasted very loudly that he wanted to ask me a few questions. Well, I asked *him* a few. I asked him if he thought there was an absolute difference between right and wrong? He said, "Yes." "Well," I said, "then you ought to take your stand upon the right to follow it wherever it carries you. Will you do it?" He tried to hedge, but I held him to it, and finally he said, "Yes." Then I asked him if he knew that there was no God, or if he knew that God did not answer prayer. He replied, "No, I do not know it. In fact I think there is a Supreme Being." But he added that he did not believe that this Supreme Being answered prayer. "Well, do you *know* He does not answer prayer?" I asked. "No," he replied, "I do not know that He does not." "Well," I said, "I know that He does, but I do not ask you to take my word for it. Try it for yourself. Here is a possible clue. It may be that God answers prayer. If you are honest, as you say you are, in your search for truth, you will try this clue, and find what there may be in it. Will you pray this prayer: O God, if there is any God, show me if Jesus Christ is Your Son or not, and if You will show me that He is, I promise to accept Him as my Savior and to confess Him as such before the world?"

He tried now to hedge and crawl more than ever. He wanted to ask me what life was, and a lot of irrelevant questions. But I held him to the point. I showed him that he did not dare to pray. At last in desperation, he got down on his knees and in his excitement kicked over a chair in doing it, and blurted out the words of a prayer. "Now," I said, "will you just take the gospel of John and read it honestly looking for light, and come back in two weeks and tell me the result?" "Yes, I will," he said. But he never came back. Why not? You know. He did not want to be cured of his unbelief. He wanted unbelief because he wanted sin.

But many *did* come back, and they all came back cured. I have been making substantially this same offer for many years now in many cities, in many states and in many lands and there has never been a single case of failure yet. Never a man yet has come back who has been able to tell me that he had taken the remedy and remained a skeptic still. Now, if you doubt that cure, try it yourself.

III. Christ Jesus Is a Cure for Poverty

The third evil I desire to refer to is poverty. ***Christ Jesus is the cure for poverty.*** Now I stand with Henry George when he says poverty is an evil. Men may get good out of poverty—many men have gotten good out of poverty; but nevertheless poverty is an evil. It is all very well for philosophers like Seneca, whom Ingersoll lauded and exalted above Paul and Jesus Christ, to write about the excellences of poverty when they themselves are squandering, as Seneca himself did, vast fortunes in the most extravagant luxury. Such "philosophy" may suit a reckless discharger of verbal pyrotechnics such as Colonel Ingersoll was, but it will not suit honest, thinking people who love their kind and keep their eyes open. Poverty is an evil.

When I walk through the homes of the very poor in various cities of this and other countries, when I see the crowding, when I breathe the poisonous air, when I hear the curses and oaths and obscenity that greet the ears of the innocent children of the poor from the day they open their eyes upon this world to the day they are carried out to the Potters' Field, when I hear and see these things, I feel like saying, "Cursed be poverty." Poverty is an evil, and I hate it. Hate it not only for myself but hate it for the sake of those who suffer from it. I cannot walk among the homes of the poor without a heartache; and I do not wish to. *Poverty is an evil: Jesus Christ is the cure.*

1. Jesus Christ is the cure for poverty with the individual.

(A.) *Jesus Christ is the cure for poverty in the life that now is.* There is no guarantee that if a man comes to Christ, he will become a man of wealth in this present life. That is not desirable for most men. Indeed there are very few men who have great wealth in the life that now is who are not spoiled by it. But there is a guarantee that if one comes to Christ, really believing in Him as Savior, and surrendering absolutely to Him as Lord and Master, their every real need will be supplied. Jesus Christ Himself said in Matthew 6:33, *"But seek ye first the kingdom of God, and his righteousness; and all these things shall be added unto you."* And the *"all these things"* are the things spoken of in the verses immediately preceding: food, drink, and clothing, and the necessities of daily life. This statement of Jesus Christ is true. I have watched the testing of it under particularly trying circumstances for forty years, and I have never known a case of failure. I have known cases of seeming failure, but when examined into fully, I have found that the failure was not in the promise of God but in those to whom the promise was unavailing, simply because they did not meet the conditions of the promise. Paul said in Philippians 4:19, *"My God shall supply every need of yours according to his riches in glory in Christ Jesus"* (ASV). That great promise is also true, *when you meet the conditions stated in the context.* I have seen these promises tested again and again in the most unpromising circumstances and neither of them has ever failed. It has seemed oftentimes as if they were going to fail, but they never have.

How many people I have known who were in the most abject poverty who have attained positions of comfort and plenty through accepting Jesus Christ. A multitude of them go trooping by in my memory as I speak. All over the city of Chicago and all over the country, there are people who have been lifted from poverty to plenty and affluence by the influence of one church, the Moody Church in Chicago. Not that this church has given them money, but the church has brought them to Christ, and Christ has brought them to plenty. The same is true of many churches throughout the land. As a matter of demonstrated fact, Jesus Christ is the cure for poverty with the individual.

(B.) *But Christ Jesus is the cure for poverty with the individual not only in the life that now is but still more abundantly in the life which is to come.* The man or woman who accepts Jesus Christ by that act becomes a child of God, and if a child then an heir, an heir of God and joint heir with Christ. (See John 1:12; Romans 8:17.) If the poorest beggar in the land were to accept Jesus Christ, that beggar would become at once an heir to estates before whose magnificence all the multimillionaires in the land fade into utter insignificance. I pass by and behold the mansions of the rich in many cities, I enter and go through the magnificent palaces of kings and emperors, as I have done in many lands; and I say all this is nothing, nothing at all to what I am soon to have.

Oh! I invite all to riches untold. There is for the child of God just a little way ahead *"an inheritance incorruptible, and undefiled, and that fadeth not away"* (1 Peter 1:4 ASV).

2. *But Jesus Christ is not only the cure for poverty in the individual. He is also the cure for poverty in society at large.* How earnestly and fruitlessly social philosophers have sought for a cure for poverty. I think Henry George has come the nearest of anyone to hitting upon a cure that would be effective and practicable. But I confess I do not expect to ever see it put into operation in the large way it would be necessary to put it into operation to have it accomplish any real and permanent good. And even if it were put into operation, I would not expect to see all the results that its more sanguine supporters imagine would follow. There would be poverty still, because there

would still be cunning greed on the one side and improvidence and laziness and waste on the other side. But when Jesus comes again to reign, He will banish poverty. Love will reign. "The lion and the lamb will lie down together" (see Isaiah 11:6), and the lamb will not be inside the lion, as is now so often the case. No more poverty, no more oppression, no more commercial warfare, no more brigandage of the strong robbing the weak, when Christ Jesus comes. Equality, fraternity, and plenty will reign everywhere.

People ask me why I long for the coming again of Jesus Christ. I long for the speedy coming of Jesus Christ for many reasons. But for one reason, because, when I go out and see the poor thousands, and tens of thousands in the great cities of our land, when I see the human hogs that dominate so much of the business and politics and society of our day, and trample the weak under their feet and into the mud in their gluttonous desire to get at their swill, I feel like crying, "How long, O Lord, how long? Come, Lord Jesus. Come quickly." This is my only hope for those who are underneath in the present mad scramble that we call business. But that is an all-sufficient hope. *He is coming!* and when He comes society will be reconstructed from the bottom up, and the principle that governs human life will no longer be "competition"—that is, to put it in plain language, "every man for himself and the devil take the hindmost"—but when He comes the governing principle of all society will be "love your neighbor as yourself," and poverty and want and oppression will then be no more forever.

Jesus Christ is the cure for poverty. If you wish to see poverty done away with enlist in the army of Christ Jesus.

IV. Christ Jesus Is the Cure for Sickness

The next evil is sickness. Some people consider sickness a blessing, and God undoubtedly does make a blessing out of sickness to some of us. I have had sicknesses and pains for which I have thanked God. But if I read my Bible right, sickness was a curse, and it belongs properly to the devil's kingdom and not God's. And I notice that most of the people who consider sickness a blessing are perfectly willing that the other fellow should enjoy all the blessings of this kind; and, if the blessing does chance to come their way, they are willing to take all kinds of bitter pills and nauseating potions to rid themselves of this highly esteemed blessing. In plain, unvarnished English, sickness is a great evil. *Jesus Christ is the cure for sickness.*

1. *Jesus Christ is the cure for sickness in this present life.* The general rule of God regarding His children is that God wishes them to be well, and Christ Jesus makes them well when they trust Him to do it. I am not going into the fine and disputed points about divine healing and the faith cure, but I know from personal experience and from a wide and careful observation extending over many years that the Lord Jesus Christ who Himself was raised from the dead, and ascended to the right hand of the Father, and has today all power in heaven and on earth, does cure sickness today. Jesus Christ, the risen Son of God, has cured many a man and woman who has been hopelessly sick for years and whom all physicians failed to heal.

2. *But it is in the life to come that the fullness of Christ's healing power will be manifested.* God's dearest and purest and noblest children do sicken and die in the life that now is, but in that life that lies just a little ways ahead there will be no death, no sickness, and no pain. There will be, however, in that other world for those who reject Christ in this world, plenty of sickness, and plenty of pain, and eternal death—endless dying. Oh, sick one, come to Jesus. He is the cure for sickness.

Time fails me to mention other evils such as bereavement, disappointment, bitterness of heart, despair, death, for which Jesus and Jesus only is the cure. *Christ Jesus is the cure for every evil known to man.* He stands tonight with outstretched hands as He did that day in Capernaum of old when He uttered the words of our text. And He calls to us as He did to them, "***Come unto me,*** *all ye that labour and are heavy laden,* ***and I will give you rest.*** *Take my yoke upon you, and learn of me; for I am meek and lowly in heart: and ye shall find rest unto your souls. For my yoke is easy and my burden is light.*"

12

JESUS IS THE CHRIST, THE SON OF GOD

"These are written, that ye may believe that Jesus is the Christ, the Son of God; and that believing ye may have life in his name."
—John 20:31 ASV

My subject tonight is Jesus is the Christ, the Son of God. You will find the text in John 20:31: *"These are written, that ye may believe that Jesus is the Christ, the Son of God; and that believing ye may have life in his name"* (ASV).

Our text declares that Jesus is the Christ, the Son of God, and that everyone who really believes that fact obtains eternal life by so believing. Listen to the text again: *"These are written, that ye may believe that Jesus is the Christ, the Son of God; and that believing ye may have life in his name."*

1. How Do We Know That Jesus Is the Christ, the Son of God?

1. *We know that Jesus is the Christ, the Son of God, by a careful and candid study of the gospel of John.* John said, "*These* **are written**, *that ye may believe that Jesus is the Christ, the Son of God; and that believing ye may have life in his name.*" In other words, John, in his gospel, presented the evidence that Jesus is the Christ, the Son of God. We do not have time to take up that evidence in detail tonight, nor do we need to. Any of you may take it up for yourselves, and if you will read the evidence as John presented it candidly—that is, read it with a sincere desire to know the truth and with an earnest determination to obey the truth when discovered—you will know to a certainty, before you get through the gospel, that Jesus is the Christ, the Son of God. I challenge any man to study the gospel of John with a candid mind, with a sincere desire to know the truth and willingness to obey it when it is found, and to come to any other conclusion than that beyond a peradventure Jesus is the very Christ of God, and the very Son of God. I have seen men try it again and again, many that were skeptics or even thoroughgoing agnostics, when they began. In every case where any man has pursued that study with a mind eager to know the truth and a willingness to obey the truth at any cost, that man has become a believer that Jesus is the Christ, the Son of God, by the time he completed the gospel. The result has been the same in every instance. Every one of them has come to see that Jesus is the Christ, the Son of God, and by believing in Him as such, has obtained eternal life. I suppose I could stand here by the hour and tell you of specific instances that have come under my own personal observation. Let me give you only one.

When I was holding meetings in Wellington, New Zealand, I spoke at the noon hour in one of the theaters to business and professional men. At the close of one of these meetings, a prominent travelling man came to me—he was said to be the most prominent travelling man in New Zealand.

He said to me, "Charlie George [one of the proprietors of the leading department store in the city] thinks I ought to have a talk with you, but you can't help me."

"What is the trouble?" I asked.

"I am an agnostic, and you can't help me."

"Well," I said, "I have helped a good many agnostics, and perhaps I can help you." Then, I continued, "What do you believe anyhow?"

He said, "I don't believe anything."

I said, "Do you not believe that there is an absolute difference between right and wrong?"

"Oh, yes, I do believe that."

"Well," I said, "you do believe something after all. That is all that I believed to begin with, and that is enough for anyone to believe to begin with." Then, I said to him, "If you have some of anything and want more, what do you do?"

"Why," he said, "I use what I have."

I said, "That is right. If you have some muscle, and want more muscle, what do you do?"

"I use the muscle I have."

"If you have some memory and want a better memory, what do you do?"

"I use the memory I have."

"If you have some money and want more money, what do you do?"

"I use the money I have."

"All right," I said, "you have some faith. You believe there is an absolute difference between right and wrong. You want more. Will you use what you have? You say you believe that there is an absolute difference between right and wrong. Will you use that faith? Will you take your stand upon the right to follow it wherever it carries you, at any cost?"

With a little hesitation, he said, "Yes, I will do that, but you can't help me. You are just wasting your time."

"Now," I said, "do you know that there is no God?"

"No," he replied, "I don't know there is no God. I don't know anything about it."

"Well," I said, "I know that there is a God, but that won't do you any good. Do you know that God does not answer prayer?"

"No, I don't know that God doesn't answer prayer. I don't believe that He does, but I don't know that He doesn't."

"Well," I said, "I know that He does, but that won't do you any good, but you know the method of modern science. The method of modern science is this—that whenever you find a possible clue to knowledge, you follow that clue out to find out what there may be in it. You don't have to know that there is anything in it. You simply follow it out to find out what there may be in it."

"Yes," he said, "that is right."

"Well, now," I said, "are you willing to apply this method of modern science to religious investigation? Will you admit that there may be a God and it may be that He answers prayer? Here then is a possible clue to knowledge. Will you follow it out to find out what there may be in it? Will you pray this prayer, 'Oh, God, if there is any God, show me if Jesus Christ is Your Son or not, and if You show me that He is, I promise to accept Him as my Savior and confess Him as such before the world.'"

"Yes," he said in a half laughing way, "I'll do that too, but it won't do any good; you can't help me. You are just wasting your time."

"Well," I replied, "I have helped a good many and perhaps I can help you. Now, just one thing more. John said in John 20:31, '*These are written, that ye may believe that Jesus is the Christ, the Son of God; and that believing ye may have life in his name.*' Now," I said, "John presented you in his gospel the evidence that Jesus is the Christ, the Son of God. Will you take the evidence and read it? I don't ask you to believe it. I don't want you even to try to believe it. I simply want you to be willing to be convinced. Will you take the gospel and read it with an open mind?"

"Oh," he said, "I have read it."

"Yes," I said, "but I want you to read it a new way. Begin at the first chapter and the first verse and read on verse after verse until you finish the gospel. Don't read too many verses at any one time. Pay careful attention to what you read and each time before you read, offer this prayer—'Oh, God, if there is any God, show me what of truth there is in these verses I am about to read and what You show me to be true, I promise to take my stand upon.'"

Rather languidly and wearily he said, "Yes, I will do that, too, but it won't do any good."

Then, I went over what he had agreed to do and got him to promise me he would write me the result.

Several weeks passed. I left Wellington and had gone to Christ Church and from Christ Church to Dunedin. After I had been a few days in Dunedin, a lady called at the house where I was stopping and asked to see me. When I entered the reception room, she arose and walked toward me with a letter in her hand, which she held out to me. She said, "I have a letter from my husband and it is the queerest letter I ever received. I don't understand it, but he said

I could show it to you." She handed me the letter and I took it and read it. It was from this man. It began:

> My dear wife,
>
> I think I have been converted. I am not sure yet, and I don't wish you to tell anyone until I am sure, but you can show this letter to your pastor and to Dr. Torrey; for it was he who spoke to me in Wellington.

That man came out clear cut as a Christian, as a believer in Jesus as the Christ, the Son of God, and in the Bible as the Word of God, and when we got to England, his mother, who was a very prominent woman in public life in England, wrote to Mr. Alexander to thank us for what we had done for her son in New Zealand. Any one of you can try it for yourself. The result always has been the same and always will be the same. There has never been an exception.

2. *We know that Jesus is the Christ, the Son of God, because that is what Jesus Himself claimed to be, and God set the stamp of His endorsement on Jesus Christ's claim by raising Him from the dead.* That Jesus claimed to be the Christ, the Son of God, the Son of God in an entirely unique sense, in a sense that no other man who ever walked this earth was the Son of God, admits of no honest question. In Mark 12:6, our Lord Jesus draws a contrast between Himself and all the prophets of the old dispensation, even the greatest, and says that while they were servants and merely servants, He was the Son, the one and only Son of God. (See Revised Version.) In John 10:30, Jesus went so far as to say, *"I and my Father are one."* In John 14:9, He even dared to say, *"He that hath seen me hath seen the Father."* In John 5:23, He went so far as to say, *"All men should honour the Son,* ***even as they honour the Father.****"* Such was Jesus' oft-repeated claim. This was a stupendous claim to make. If the claim was not true, it was an utterly and shamefully blasphemous

claim. The Jews put Jesus Christ to death on a charge of blasphemy for making this claim. And if this claim of Jesus was not true, if Jesus was not the Christ, the Son of God, the Son of God in a sense that no other is the Son of God, then the Jews did right, according to their own God-given law, in putting Him to death on the charge of blasphemy, only they should have put Him to death by stoning and not by crucifixion. You cannot deny the deity of Jesus without thereby justifying the Jews in putting Him to death. If you are a Unitarian, and are also logical, you must justify the putting to death of Jesus Christ. But before the Jewish authorities put Him to death, Jesus said to them that God would set the stamp of His endorsement upon His claim for which they were putting Him to death, by raising Him from the dead. Put Him to death they did. Lay Him in Joseph's sepulcher they did. Roll the stone to the door of the sepulcher they did. Seal the stone with the Roman seal, which to break was death, they did. But when the appointed hour came, just as Jesus had foretold, the quickening breath of God swept through that sleeping clay, and God raised Him triumphant over death and grave, and so proclaimed to all coming generations, and to us, more clearly than if He should proclaim it from the open heavens above Los Angeles tonight, "This man is what He claimed to be; He is the Christ, He is the Son of God, He is very God of very God, all men should honor Him even as they honor Me, the Father." I have proven time and time again from this platform that the resurrection of Jesus from the dead is the best proven fact of history; and the absolutely certain resurrection of the Lord Jesus Christ proves to a demonstration that He is the Christ, the Son of God, very God of very God.

3. *We know that Jesus is the Christ, the Son of God, by His influence upon all subsequent history.* That Jesus Christ claimed to be the Christ, the Son of God, in an entirely unique sense admits, as we have already seen, of no honest question; but that Jesus claimed to be the Christ, the Son of God, a divine person to be honored and

worshipped, even as God the Father is honored and worshipped, does not prove that He really was so. But it does prove that He either was the Son of God in an entirely unique sense, as He claimed to be, or else that He was the most daring and blasphemous and outrageous impostor that ever walked this earth, or else that He was one of the most hopeless lunatics that ever disgraced humanity by his mental imbecility. The modern Unitarian position, the position also of some preachers who do not call themselves Unitarians but orthodox and evangelical, that Jesus was not a divine person, very God of very God, that He was the Son of God only in the sense that we are all sons of God, but that He was a good man, perhaps the best man who ever lived on this earth, is the very acme of irrationality and intellectual absurdity. Whatever Jesus was, He was not a good man; that is to say, if He were not God as He claimed to be, He was not good, but one of the most outrageous impostors or one of the most hopeless lunatics that ever walked this earth. Now let me put to each one of you a question. Was the influence of Jesus of Nazareth upon subsequent history the influence of an impostor? Only one whose own heart is cankered by imposture and fraud would think for one moment of asserting it. Let me ask you a second question, Was the influence of Jesus of Nazareth upon subsequent history the influence of a lunatic? Only a lunatic would venture to assert it. Here then we are—not a lunatic, not an impostor, then beyond question, the Christ, the Son of God, God manifest in the flesh.

4. *We know that Jesus is the Christ, the Son of God, by the divine power that He displays today.* Jesus displayed divine power when He was here on earth. He displayed divine power when He stilled the tempest and calmed the waves by His word, saying, *"Peace, be still"* (Mark 4:39), and there was a great calm. He displayed divine power when He called Lazarus, who had been four days dead, from the grave and Lazarus came forth. He displayed divine power when He turned water into wine. He displayed divine power when

He fed five thousand men, besides women and children, with five small loaves and two small fishes and had more left over when He was through than when He began, which was a creative act. Over and over again He displayed divine power when He was here on earth. But we do not need to go way back into the history of His life here upon earth, nearly 1,900 years ago, to find Him displaying divine power. He displays divine power today. He raises the dead today. He raises men and women who are dead in trespasses and sins into spiritual life and power and victory. He does something far more wonderful than turning water into wine. He turns outrageous sinners into glorious saints.

He turned a Jerry McAuley, a miserable, contemptible, low-down river thief, an inmate of Sing Sing States Prison, into Jerry McAuley, the apostle of life to the outcasts of New York; so honored when he came to die in the very city where he had been a water thief, that the best people of New York gathered by the thousands at his funeral to do honor to his blessed memory. He turned Sam Hadley, a fugitive from justice, with 138 counts for forgery out against him, and a hopeless barrelhouse bum, into Sam Hadley, one of the most lovable men and self-sacrificing lovers of his fellowmen I ever knew, and whom I once met in Washington as the honored guest in the home of the U.S. Postmaster General. He turned William S. Jacoby, a drunkard at nine, a tough at fifteen, a criminal at nineteen, and a companion of thugs, a desperado in Omaha, twice dishonorably discharged from the regular army, invited to join the Jesse James Gang, unanimously chosen chief of a gang of desperados in the Leavenworth Federal Prison, riding through the streets of Omaha firing his revolver out of the window of a cab at everything he passed, into the Rev. William S. Jacoby, the most loved man in Chicago, the dearest and truest friend I ever had, and the most truly Christlike man I ever knew. Yes, and He changed me. I will not tell you from what; but at least from hopeless bondage to glorious liberty, and from awful death to exultant life. Yes,

Jesus is surely the Christ, the Son of God, very God of very God. There is no possibility of honest and intelligent doubt of that.

II. The Result of Believing That Jesus Is the Christ, the Son of God

Now let us look at the result of believing that Jesus is the Christ, the Son of God. If one believes that Jesus is the Christ, the Son of God, what will be the result? Listen to my text again—*"These are written, that ye may believe that Jesus is the Christ, the Son of God; and that believing ye may have life in his name."*

1. *The result will be that the one who believes that Jesus is the Christ, the Son of God, will obtain eternal life.* All that anyone needs to do to obtain eternal life, that greatest of all gifts, a gift in comparison with which all the wealth, splendor, honor, glory, and pleasure of this world are as nothing, the gift of eternal life, all that any one has to do to obtain this wondrous gift is to believe that Jesus is the Christ, the Son of God. Anyone in this audience may have eternal life in the twinkling of an eye by just believing that Jesus is the Christ, the Son of God. Listen again to our text, *"These are written, **that ye may believe** that Jesus is the Christ, the Son of God; **and that believing ye may have life in his name.**"* Listen to another verse: John 3:16, *"For God so loved the world, that he gave his only begotten Son, that **whosoever believeth in him** should not perish, but **have everlasting life.**"* You may be a drunkard. You may be a thief. You may be an embezzler. You may be a forger. You may be a man or woman who is disgraced by divorce, and you yourself the guilty party. You may be an outrageous blasphemer. You may have a polluted imagination and a rotten heart. You may be the victim of the lowest and vilest passions that ever cursed a man or woman. You may be anybody or anything. But *believe that Jesus is the Christ, the Son of God, and eternal life is instantly yours.* Oh, how often I have

seen men and women, of all kinds and conditions and nationalities, get eternal life in an instant by simply believing that Jesus is the Christ, the Son of God.

2. *But, of course, it must be real faith.* The faith that John spoke of here is not a mere intellectual opinion; John never used "faith" in that sense. No man ever obtained eternal life by merely having an orthodox opinion about Jesus. When Jesus Himself was here on earth, the demons held a perfectly orthodox opinion about Him. They cried out (even before men saw it and confessed it), *"I know thee who thou art, **the Holy One of God**"* (Mark 1:24; Luke 4:34). The devil himself holds a perfectly orthodox opinion about Christ. He knows, and only too well for his own comfort, that Jesus is the Christ, the Son of God. He does not teach it, but he knows it. He gets men to teach that Jesus is not the Christ, the Son of God, very God of very God, because *"he is a liar, and the father of it"* (John 8:44). He gets men to teach that Jesus is a good man, that He is a great example, but that He is not divine, that He does not save by the shedding of His blood but by His example and His teaching; for the devil is, as I say, a liar, and the father of it. All the time, the devil knows that Jesus is the Christ, the Son of God. He knows that someday he will himself be forced to bow his knee to Jesus and *"confess that Jesus Christ is Lord to the glory of God the Father"* (Philippians 2:11). Yes, the devil believes in that sense that Jesus is the Christ, the Son of God, but that belief does not save him from going to the everlasting fire prepared for him and his angels. No, the faith that saves is real faith, a faith with the heart. As Paul put it in Romans 10:9–10, *"If thou shalt confess with thy mouth Jesus as Lord, and shalt **believe in thy heart** that God raised him from the dead, thou shalt be saved: for **with the heart** man **believeth** unto righteousness, and with the mouth confession is made unto salvation"* (ASV).

What is heart faith, real faith, saving faith, eternal-life-giving faith? Heart faith, real faith, saving faith, eternal-life-giving faith is the faith that not only enlightens the mind but governs the will and the feelings and the conduct. It is the faith that leads to action in accordance with the truth believed. To believe with the heart that Jesus is the Christ, the Son of God, will lead you to act in accordance with the fact that Jesus is the Christ, the Son of God. The word *Christ* is really a Greek word and means "anointed One." It means just the same as the Hebrew word *Messiah*. It means "anointed King." To believe with the heart that Jesus is the Christ will lead you to enthrone Jesus as King in your heart and to surrender the whole control and conduct of your life to Him. And to believe *with the heart* that Jesus is the Son of God will lead you to surrender every thought to His control: so that if the whole world of German "scholarship" and English "scholarship" and Scotch "scholarship" and American "scholarship" were to say one thing and the Lord Jesus were to say another, you would believe Jesus against the whole crowd. If the great and widely-respected Dean Shaler Matthews and the scholarly Professor Case and a whole bevy of self-styled "scholars," some of whom have more degrees after their names than they have real sound sense in their heads and humility in their hearts, were to say one thing, and they do, and Jesus Christ were to say another thing, and they admit that He does, I would believe the glorious Son of God against the whole pretentious but pitiable pack. And if you believe with your heart that Jesus is the Christ, the Son of God, you will accept Him as your divine Savior, who purchased forgiveness for you by dying in your place on the cross, for that is what He said He did (see Matthew 20:28), and your risen Savior who, by His resurrection power, can set you free from the power of sin today, for that is what He Himself offers to do. (See John 8:34–36.) Once more, if you believe that Jesus is the Christ, the Son of God, you will bow down before Him and honor Him, even as you honor God the Father. You will worship Him as the divine person He claims to be and that you know Him to be. You will do exactly what Thomas did when at last after many stubborn doubts he was brought by seeing the risen Christ to believe that Jesus was the Christ, the Son of God. You will fall down upon your knees and look up into His blessed, glorious, divine face and cry to Him, "*My Lord and my God*" (John 20:28), and you will obtain eternal life the moment you do. Will you do it?

13

WHOM SHALL WE BELIEVE: GOD OR MAN?

"For what if some did not believe? shall their unbelief make the faith of God without effect? God forbid: yea, let God be true, but every man a liar."
—Romans 3:3–4

What I shall say tonight will save some of you, eternally and gloriously save you. But alas! It will lead to the eternal doom and destruction of some of you. It will save some of you because you will listen to the truth, and in consequence of your listening attentively and honestly to the truth, you will take the steps tonight that will lead to your salvation right here and now. But what I shall say tonight will lead to the eternal doom and destruction of some of you; because you will not listen to the truth, but harden your hearts against it and reject it, and thus this very sermon that might have saved you, if you had heeded it, will come up against you in the Day of Judgment. Truth heeded saves; truth rejected damns. Our Lord Jesus said in John 12:48, "*He that rejecteth me, and receiveth not my words, hath one that judgeth him:* ***the word that I have spoken****, the same shall judge him in the last day.*"

And the truth I am to present tonight has in it a distinctive saving power if you will only heed it and believe it and obey it. It also has in it distinctive power to bring condemnation and doom and destruction to those who refuse to heed it and thereby reject it.

I. God's Word Better than Man's

We live in a day when men are disposed to put great faith in what men say, especially what learned men say, but very little faith or no faith at all in what God says. Let some great man of science announce some discovery, and no matter how astonishing or even incredible that discovery may seem to be, no matter how much there is about it that we cannot understand, we believe it at once. But let a man find something in the Word of God that is contrary to his preconceived notions, or outside his own experience, or that has something in it that he cannot understand, or something that for one reason or another appears incredible at the first glance, he discards it at once. Tell men what great men say, and they accept it at once: tell men what the Bible says, and they look wise and shrug their shoulders and say, "Yes, but I don't think so. This is what I think." And yet tell them what some great scientist or some leading literary critic or some brilliant but erratic preacher says, and they think that settles it, that it must be so. What utter foolishness! The opinion of the greatest scientist that ever lived, or the greatest philosopher, or the most learned Hebrew or Greek scholar, or the most brilliant pulpit orator is of no value whatever against the Word of the infinitely wise and eternally truthful God, against the Word of the "*God,* ***who cannot lie***" (Titus 1:2) and who is never mistaken. The opinion of all the wise men on earth is of no weight whatever against the Word of God. One short sentence from God's sure Word is worth whole volumes of man's vain speculations, *"let God be true, and every man a liar."* The man who believes any man against God is a fool. The man who believes any company of men against God is a fool. The man who believes God against the whole world is a truly wise man.

The Bible is the Word of God. That can be proven by many unanswerable proofs. I have proven it time and time again from this platform. For eighteen centuries and more, the opinions of scientists and philosophers have come and gone, today regarded as the final and absolute wisdom, tomorrow regarded as sheerest folly. But the teachings of this Book have stood fast amid the wreck of centuries of man's thinking. The experience of eighteen centuries proves that the man who banks on the Bible is wise. The man who throws the Bible overboard at any point and turns to any other source of "light and leading" always misses it. He always has missed it for eighteen centuries; he always will miss it for all the centuries to come. The truly wise man is the man who always believes this Book against any man, against any scientist, against any philosopher, against any literary scholar, against any council of theologians or any congress of philosophers and savants. If the Bible says one thing and any man on earth says another, every truly wise man will say, *"Let God be true, and every man a liar."*

II. Some Points on which Many Great Men Differ with God

Let me call your attention to some points on which many great men and God differ.

1. *Many great and scholarly men differ from God regarding the existence of a personal devil.* A very large number of men in our

day, including some great thinkers and even some theologians of high repute, laugh at the very idea of there being any such person as the devil. Many men have said, "There is no devil but sin." And Mrs. Mary Baker Eddy who has a great following, including many people of intelligence and culture, ridicules the idea of there being a personal devil. Now that is what many men say, very many men say, many men whom you and I would be disposed to listen to on many subjects, "There is no personal devil."

What does God say? Turn in your Bible to Ephesians 6:11–12, and you will see for yourselves exactly what God says: "*Put on the whole armor of God, that ye may be able to stand against the wiles of* ***the devil.*** *For our wrestling is not against flesh and blood, but against the principalities, against the powers, against the world-rulers of this darkness, against the spiritual hosts of wickedness in the heavenly places*" (ASV). Four verses further, God says, "*Withal taking up the shield of faith, wherewith ye shall be able to quench all the fiery darts of* ***the evil one***" (not of evil, mind you, but "*the evil one*"). Now turn to 1 Peter 5:8 and you will see again what God says, "*Be sober, be watchful; your adversary the* ***devil,*** *as a roaring lion, walketh about, seeking whom he may devour*" (ASV).

There can be no doubt about the meaning of these words by anyone who reads them with the purpose of finding out what they were intended to teach and not merely with the purpose of distorting and twisting them to fit into his own preconceived notions. So we see that God says in the most unmistakable terms, that *there is a personal devil.* Furthermore, God says that the devil is a being of such great cunning and great power; that he is more than a match for you or me; and that he is plotting our destruction and all the time working to compass it. Is God right about this? Or are Mrs. Eddy and the others who deny the existence of a personal devil right? God is right about it. Certainly God is right about it. *God is always right: and any man or woman who differs from God is always wrong.* When you believe that there is no devil but your own sins, you are a sorely deceived individual; and the very devil you do not think exists has deceived you, and he has done it in order to destroy you. An enemy in ambush is a particularly dangerous enemy. And a devil who has persuaded people that he does not exist at all is a particularly dangerous devil. No class of people fall so easy a prey to the devil's subtlety as the people who do not believe that there is any devil. Show me a man or woman who does not believe that there is any devil, and I will show you every time a man or woman whom the devil has blinded and upon whom he is getting in his work.

2. *Many men differ from God regarding a future judgment.* Many men in this day, yes, very many men, do not believe that there is to be a future judgment. Tell many men of our day that there is a time coming when they shall have to stand before the judgment bar of God, with His holy and all-seeing eye piercing them through and through, and answer to Him for all their deeds done in the body, and all their words spoken in this present life. Tell them that, and they will laugh at you in derision.

But what does God say? Turn to Acts 17:30–31, and see what He said through Paul to a group of Epicurean and Stoic philosophers gathered on the historic Areopagus. "*God...now...commandeth men that they should all everywhere repent: inasmuch as* ***he hath appointed a day, in the which he will judge the world in righteousness*** *by the man whom he hath ordained; whereof he hath given assurance unto all men, in that he hath raised him from the dead*" (ASV). Turn to Romans 14:12 and read what God says about it, "*So then every one of us shall give account of himself to God.*" Turn to 2 Corinthians 5:10 and read what God says, "*We must all be made manifest before the judgment-seat of Christ; that each one may receive the things done in the body, according to what he hath done, whether it be good or bad*" (ASV). Turn to Matthew 12:36, and read what God says, "*I say unto you, that every idle word that men shall speak, they shall give account thereof in the day of judgment.*" Can anything be plainer than God's Word on this point? Is God right or are these learned gentlemen who differ from God right? God is right, and these men who differ from God are wrong. God is always right and men are always wrong when they differ from God.

There is one thing concerning the future that is absolutely sure. It is absolutely sure that there will be a judgment day. It is not absolutely sure that you or I will live another day. I saw a neighbor of mine walking down the street the day before yesterday. This morning, just before I came here, another neighbor came in and told me this first neighbor died at ten minutes before ten last night. It is not absolutely sure that there will be another election or another Christmas. It is not absolutely sure that there will be times of peace right ahead of us or times of great conflict. It is not absolutely sure what will be the outcome of the great Peace Conference now being held in Washington upon which the attention of the better part of the civilized world is now focused. But *it is absolutely sure that there will be a Judgment Day.* It is sure that you and I will stand before the judgment seat of Christ to give account of the deeds done in the body and the words spoken in the life that now is. It is absolutely sure that "*each one of us shall give account of himself to God.*"

3. *Many men, including men who are accorded wise by the world, differ from God regarding hell.*

(A.) There are many in our day who do not believe that there is to be any hell at all in the world to come. There are many able and scholarly men who say, "There is no hell except the hell a man makes for himself in the life that now is, the hell of his own tormenting conscience, and the hell of troubles arising from his own misdoings." An intelligent woman said to me a while ago, "Why, Mr. Torrey, you don't believe in hell!" It is not a question of what

I believe, but of what God says. What does God say? Turn to Matthew 5:29–30, *"And if thy right eye causeth thee to stumble, pluck it out, and cast it from thee: for it is profitable for thee that one of thy members should perish, and* ***not thy whole body*** *be cast into hell. And if thy right hand causeth thee to stumble, cut it off, and cast it from thee: for it is profitable for thee that one of thy members should perish, and* ***not thy whole body go into hell"*** (ASV). Turn to Luke 12:4–5 and read what God says: *"Be not afraid of them that kill the body, and after that have no more that they can do. But I will warn you whom ye shall fear: Fear him, who after he hath killed, hath power to cast into hell; yea, I say unto you, Fear him"* (ASV). Turn to the last book in the Bible and read what God says. *"But for the fearful, and unbelieving, and abominable, and murderers, and fornicators, and sorcerers, and idolaters, and all liars, their part shall be* ***in the lake that burneth with fire and brimstone; which is the second death"*** (Revelation 21:8 ASV).

(B.) Then there are many who believe that there is to be a future hell, but they do not believe it will be everlasting. Many say to me, "You don't believe in everlasting punishment, do you?" Again, I say it is not a question of what I believe or what you believe, but of what God says. Turn to Matthew 25:41 and read, *"Then shall he say also unto them on the left hand, Depart from me, ye cursed, into the eternal fire, which is prepared for the devil and his angels."* Compare that with Revelation 20:10, where we are told definitely about that fire that is prepared for the devil and his angels and about its duration. This is what we read, *"And the devil that deceived them was cast into the lake of fire and brimstone, where the beast and the false prophet are* [in the next to the closing verse of the preceding chapter compared with the preceding verse of this chapter we are told that the Beast and the false prophet had already been there a thousand years], *and shall be tormented day and night* ***for ever and ever."*** Turn to Revelation 14:9–11 and read, *"If any man worshippeth the beast and his image and receiveth a mark on his forehead, or upon his hand,* *he also shall drink of the wine of the wrath of God, which is prepared unmixed in the cup of his anger; and he shall be tormented with fire and brimstone in the presence of the holy angels, and in the presence of the Lamb: and the smoke of their torment goeth up forever and ever; and they have no rest day and night, they that worship the beast and his image and whoso receiveth the mark of his name*" (ASV). Turn once more to Revelation 20:15, where we are told plainly what will come to pass at the judgment of the great white throne, at the end of the millennium: "*And if any was not found written in the book of life, he was cast into the lake of fire*" (ASV). Is your name written in the Book of Life? If it is not you would better speed up and get it written there tonight, or you will spend an endless eternity in hell. I do not state that as my own opinion. I declare it as God's Word plainly set forth in His Book.

4. *Not a few wise men, as the world counts wisdom, not a few prominent theologians, differ from God about a future probation.* There are many men, oftentimes men whom the world considers very wise, who say with great positivity that if men do not repent of their sins and accept Jesus Christ now in this life, they will get another chance to repent and turn to Christ after they have died. I used to believe that myself. But what does God say? Turn to John 8:21. Read for yourself what God says through the lips of His Son, who spoke the very words of God, "*He said therefore again unto them, I go away, and ye shall seek me,* ***and shall die in your sin: whither I go, ye cannot come***" (ASV). Here the Lord Jesus speaking for God declares in the plainest kind of language that *if men die in their sin they cannot go where He goes.* Turn to Hebrews 9:27 and read what God says, "*It is appointed unto men once to die, but* ***after this the judgment.***" In these words *God plainly declares that what comes after death is not another probation but "the judgment."* If you still have any doubt as to what God says on this point, turn to 2 Corinthians 5:10, "*For we must all appear before the judgment seat of Christ; that every one may receive* ***the things done in his body,***

according to that he hath done, whether it be good or bad." Here we are distinctly told that the basis of the judgment will be the *"things done in the body,"* that is, the things done before we leave this present life, "the things done" before we "shuffle off this mortal coil," the things done while we are still in the body, the things done this side the grave. And here again God is right. God is always right and any man who differs from God is always wrong.

5. *Many men, including some of the brightest thinkers and most brilliant writers, differ from God regarding the way of salvation.* Many men say that "if a man lives a good moral life he will be saved." They say, "He may be a Jew, or a Mohammedan, or a Buddhist, or a Christian, but if he is only sincere, he will be saved just the same." They say, "No man will be lost simply because he did not believe on Jesus Christ and confess Him before the world." When I lived in Chicago, a preacher who had a very wide reputation for his ability and who claimed to be a Christian said not long after the death of Colonel Robert Ingersoll, "Heaven or any good country will welcome a man like Colonel Ingersoll." And the infidels applauded when he said it, and exclaimed, "What a broad-minded preacher," I suppose that this professedly Christian preacher was highly pleased to get the applause of the avowed enemies of Jesus Christ. But what does God say? Turn to the words of the Lord Jesus Himself in John 14:6, *"I am the way, the truth, and the life:* ***No man cometh unto the Father but by*** [through] ***me."*** Turn to Acts 4:12, *"Neither is there salvation* ***in any other:*** *for there is none other name under heaven given among men, whereby we must be saved."* Turn to John 3:18, *"He that believeth on him is not condemned: but he that believeth not is* ***condemned*** *already* ***because he hath not believed in the name of the only begotten Son of God."*** Turn to John 3:36, *"He that believeth on the Son hath everlasting life: and* ***he that believeth not the Son shall not see life;*** *but* ***the wrath of God abideth on him."*** Turn to Romans 10:9–10, *"If thou shalt* ***confess with thy mouth the Lord Jesus,*** *and* ***shalt believe in thine heart*** *that God raised him from*

the dead, ***thou shalt be saved.*** *For with the heart man believeth unto righteousness; and* ***with the mouth confession is made unto salvation.***" Turn to the words of the Lord Jesus Himself in Matthew 10:32–33, "*Whosoever therefore* ***shall confess me before men,*** *him will I confess also before my Father which is in heaven. But whosoever shall* ***deny me before men,*** *him will I also deny before my Father which is in heaven.*" There is no mistaking the meaning of these words by any man who desires to know what God's Word really does say.

6. *Many thoughtful men, including not a few professors in Methodist and other professedly Christian colleges and universities and theological seminaries, differ from God regarding the conditions of entering into the kingdom of God.* Many men say that the way to get into the kingdom of God is by leading an upright life, by treating your wife and your children well, and being honest in business, being kind to the poor, practicing "the social gospel," etc. Others say that the way to enter the kingdom of God is by being baptized, and uniting with the church, partaking of the Communion, reading the Bible, saying your prayers, going to confession, and doing other religious works. Others say that the way to enter the kingdom of God is by having a good ancestry, being carefully reared and well educated in Christian schools and colleges. But what does God say? "*Jesus answered and said unto him, Verily, verily, I say unto thee,* ***Except a man be born again,*** *he cannot see the kingdom of God....Jesus answered, Verily, verily, I say unto thee,* ***Except a man be born of water and the Spirit,*** *he cannot enter into the kingdom of God*" (John 3:3, 5). Turn to Titus 3:5, "*Not by works done in righteousness, which we did ourselves, but according to his mercy he saved us,* ***through the washing of regeneration and renewing of the Holy Spirit***" (ASV). God says that the only way to enter the kingdom and be saved is by being born again, becoming a new creation through the power of the Holy Spirit within us.

7. *Many men differ from God regarding the best time to repent and accept Christ.* Many of you here tonight differ from God concerning

that. Many men are saying that there will be someday a better time than tonight to repent of your sins and turn to Jesus Christ, and to confess Christ before the world. Many of you here tonight are saying it, or thinking it if you do not actually say it, or acting it if you do not distinctly think it. But what does God say? Second Corinthians 6:2, *"Behold, now is the acceptable time; behold, now is the day of salvation."* Listen again, Hebrews 3:7, *"The Holy Ghost saith,* ***To day*** *if ye will hear his voice"* (ASV). Listen again to Proverbs 27:1, *"Boast not thyself of tomorrow for thou knowest not what a day may bring forth."* Listen once more, Proverbs 29:1, *"He, that being often reproved hardeneth his neck, shall suddenly be destroyed, and that without remedy."* Felix, the great Roman governor of old, fancied there would be a "more convenient season" and waited for it, but he never found it. That is why he will spend eternity in hell.

These are some of the things that men say and some of the things that God says. Which will you believe? I say with Paul, *"Let God be true, and every man a liar."*

But perhaps someone here will say, "But I don't believe the Bible is the Word of God." My friend, did it ever occur to you that doubting a fact does not alter the fact? Did it ever occur to you that your not believing the Bible to be the Word of God does not alter in the least the fully proven fact that the Bible is the Word of God?

At the time of the Boxer Rebellion in China, some of the Boxers did not believe they could be killed by bullets. They thought their incantations and strange rites made them invulnerable. These men were very honest and entirely sincere about this belief. A Chinese army officer demanded that they prove their sincerity by drawing up in line that he might have his soldiers shoot at them. They immediately consented. They were very sincere. They drew up in line and fearlessly faced the firing squad. The Chinese soldiers blazed away, and the Boxers dropped dead. Their doubt of the power of bullets to kill them did not alter the fact. Your doubt that the Bible is God's Word does not alter the fact, not one iota. Suppose for a moment that the Bible turns out to be the Word of God. You must admit that there is at least a possibility that the Bible may be the Word of God. You must admit that the men and women who are really living nearest God and know God best believe the Bible is the Word of God. Suppose they prove to be right. Where then will you be? Damned. And that is just exactly what you will be if you go on doubting God's Word and rejecting God's Son, listening to the voice of men rather than to the voice of God.

God says that there is a devil and that you need Christ's help against his cunning and power; God says that there is a future judgment that we must all appear before the judgment seat of Christ to receive the things done in the body; God says that there is a hell and that it is a place of torment where all who reject Christ in the life that now is will spend eternity; God says that there is no future probation, that the issues of eternity are settled in the life that now is; God says that there is but one way to be saved, which is by accepting Jesus Christ as our Savior, surrendering ourselves to Him as our Lord, and confessing Him as such before the world; God says that the only way to enter the kingdom of God is by being born again by the power of the Holy Spirit, upon our accepting the Lord Jesus Christ. God says that the best time to accept Christ and to be saved is right *now*. *"Behold, now is the acceptable time."* The Holy Spirit sayeth today.

> *"Boast not thyself of to morrow; for thou knowest not what a day may bring forth."* (Proverbs 27:1)

> *"He that being often reproved hardeneth his neck, shall suddenly be destroyed, and that without remedy."* (Proverbs 29:1)

Who will turn from sin and unbelief and turn to Christ right now?